AF770237

ROBERT'S RULES

to Repeal & Replace

Trickle-Down Economics

ROBERT'S RULES

to Repeal & Replace Trickle-Down Economics

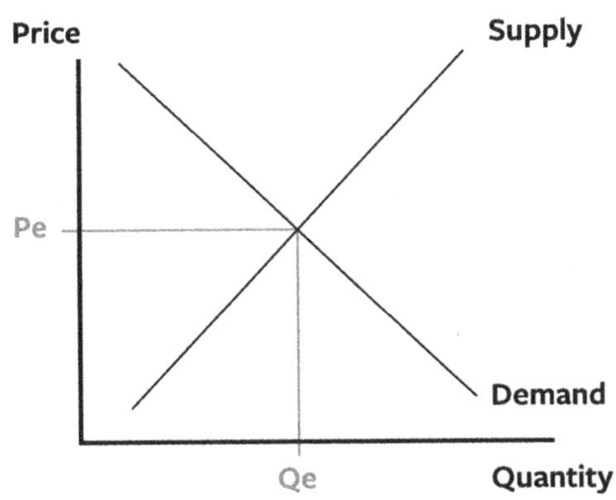

**Demand and supply curves in equilibrium*

ROBERT J. BROWN SR

Robert's Rules to Repeal & Replace Trickle-Down Economics © copyright 2020 by Robert J. Brown Sr. All rights reserved. No part of this book may be reproduced in any form whatsoever, by photography or xerography or by any other means, by broadcast or transmission, by translation into any kind of language, nor by recording electronically or otherwise, without permission in writing from the author, except by a reviewer, who may quote brief passages in critical articles or reviews.

ISBNs: 978-1-7354968-0-1 (pbk); 978-1-7354968-1-8 (ebook)

Book design by Mayfly Design

Library of Congress Catalog Number: 2020914218
First Printing: 2020

CONTENTS

PART TWO: ROBERT'S REALITIES

PART THREE: SOLUTIONS (RULE #6)

AUTHOR'S NOTE

The author would like to be very clear. It is not my intent to offend the intelligence of anyone reading this book. You need to know now, I am adamantly opposed to trickle-down economics and anyone offering it as a solution. When I say anyone, I mean anyone: republican, democrat, communist, independent, dictators, socialist, or conservative: it doesn't matter to me. When has pursuing economic hate and division ever turned up to be a good outcome for humanity? Everyone please wake up; the need to change trickle down economic policies are equivalent to our need to focus on and stop climate change (recognizing many are in denial). Trickle down capitalism is a tool of choice. Trickle down incentives and policies are negative externalities to our ability to address climate change because we allow monopoly profits and greed to be the incentives for entrepreneurs around the world. Either you understand the urgency to change what we are doing or you don't or maybe you just don't care. The author will say things to get under your skin, if it helps to get your undivided attention. For others, the color of their skin gives them the additional rights and privileges to demean others not like them.

As an economist, I am now feeling personally offended by trickle-down economic policies and all the chaos it brings to our society, and its unfair and doesn't work. I feel like I have to defend the entire economic profession against trickle-down ignorance. In the process, I have used some sharp language in confronting those that promote skewed restricted trickle-down competition. I would like to see worldwide market competition at every level, not watered down by trickle down. I want to see a lot more entrepreneurs with balance sheets that are "In The Black" circulating dollars in our own communities.

Anyone that has national ideas that include freedom, fairness, human rights, and a willingness to reach common ground, with a strength of principles, and can commit to something greater than yourself, should be interested in reading this book. This book does more than just complain about the current economic, political, and religious conditions, it will offer some real practical solutions. Our economy has to be given the right incentives to maximize employment and production. Equilibrium economics provides the world with sustainable incentives for the twenty-first century and beyond.

INTRODUCTION

We live in a world that needs diversity and inclusion. What does that mean to people of color and those in the minority? I recently heard someone sum it up quite nicely, "Ask those in the minorities to come to the party" is diversity, but "asking them to dance" once at the party is inclusion.

As for a sound economic theory, Keynesian economics is the backbone in my analysis. Keynesian theories are far more sustainable than the rich man's fixed and rigged systems offered by economists Robert Mundell and Arthur Laffer, and implemented by David Stockman that created Reaganomics and supply-side economics.

We live in the richest country in the world and we struggle to be humane to one another. Trickle-down/supply-side economics has watered down our society, our constitution, our values and our sense of fairness, all for money and power. Supply-side economic policies are not sustainable in the long-run, but wealthy Americans on both political sides, republicans and democrats, have gone back to these policies time and time again, taking money and resources from the poor and giving it to the rich. The one presidential exception to trickle-down was President Barack Obama who tried to implement "middle class economics" a form of equilibrium economics.

Supply-side economic policies polarize our society and question our beliefs about what our commitments to each other are as a society and how best to protect the wealthy. As a society we need to run away from supply-side theories that only protect wealthy individuals and implement policies that naturally stress equilibrium fairness. The policies we implement are the policies that guide the spirit and tone of our society. The supply-siders are obsessed by their greedy and very mean-spirited individuals. Supply-siders pride themselves in figuring out ways to exploit the weak in our society for personal gain. Trickle-down turns the society onto itself, like a skin or flesh eating disease, seeking profits at the expense of others. Trickle-down policies do not stimulate the society to work together to solve problems they only create profits. Trickle-down economics is all about self-interest and has nothing to do with building nations or a community. Personal greed has taken over, and now it's an eye for an eye and the society has gone blind. We have forgotten that when we are able to help the most vulnerable people in our society, our entire society becomes more humane.

For eight years, republicans were successful in polarizing and shutting down Washington when Barack Obama was elected president with their trickle-down policies of "no and hell no" to anything President Obama proposed. Republicans displayed the full-Monty in pitting/polarizing American against American, rich against the poor, people of color against white. Republicans demeaned President Obama and, in doing so, they demeaned the office of the president and the principles of democracy and countless American citizens.

Republicans prefer and elected the most polarizing/demeaning president in American history. Now we are stuck with a polarized congress that is still shut-down and can't seem to get back on track of being a world leader. We live in a society that struggles to maintain civility and the rule of law.

Equilibrium economic policies are a game changer when it comes to societal depolarization and stimulating our society toward (societal fairness), equal treatment, fairness in our marketplace, and how we're going to address the polarizing issues already in motion.

Remember, our goal is to form a more perfect union.

The same God that made you, made you and me the same. Black and White people genetically and every person of color in between, "we are identical." Do I need to say that again, "we are identical." Not just a lot alike, but genetically identical. We can educate and train young boys from the South Sudan, to become astronauts, because we are identical. We're here in the twenty-first century and the wealthy 2 percent of the population is sponsoring the pigment of our skin to polarize, divide, and isolate people into pigmented groups—the most elementary way to divide people without using any intelligence. We need to come together as a people to solve our problems.

In the United States we have this partnership between the government (public sector of society) and the private sector (large and small businesses of society) with a common goal of forming a more perfect union for the United States and its citizens. In America, the public sector has historically taken the lead in providing economic and societal fairness. Efforts to maintain societal fairness is diminishing due to greedy, ignorant, economic politicians.

This allowed the private sector to drag slowly behind. Now, trickle-down economics has reversed the roles of our society caretakers of economic/societal fairness and has given the majority of the responsibility to the private sector. A private sector of Americans that has historically proven to be uncaring and nonresponsive to our societal needs and totally focused on tax breaks for the rich, the stock market, and private personal greed. How do you think that's going to work out?

Trickle-down pressure to privatize and cut social programs is the goal that overrides economic fairness and the willingness to form a more perfect union for all US citizens. The leaders of this new attack on American fairness are the immoral Russian president, ignorant President Trump, spineless Mitch McConnell and lap-dog Paul Ryan. Three ignorant fools and Putin, that can't possibly understand the importance of forming a more perfect union or protecting the economic fairness for the United States or any society. Republicans have stolen the responsibility for providing economic fairness and they are "clueless." We are now being governed by the most inhumane, uneducated, openly racist, rich, and trashy Americans in history. They continue to take from the poor and give to the rich. When the wealthy neglect their responsibilities to society, the society becomes inhumane.

"In my opinion, large tax cuts for the top 2 percent will just go in the pockets of uncaring greedy capitalist Americans. These leeches in our society are very comfortable taking everything you give them to include the blood of hardworking Americans. Like you, they have no sense of political or economic fairness and are willing and able to change the rule of law and have no respect for the truth." (September 4, 2017, letter to Senator Mitch McConnell)

Robert's Rules of Economics

Robert's Rules of economics are common-sense rules of economics being applied to the chaos in the world. The concept of providing "socially optimal solutions" is not new. In fact, John Kenneth Galbraith wrote about it in his book *American Capitalism* in 1952.

We live in a world where the president of the United States is lying every day, full of arrogance and delusions of grandeur. He is a US president that is being used like a puppet by Putin and the republicans. Dangerous and strange bedfellows unseen before in US history. Robert's Rules of economics will get the confused screwed-up American heads screwed back on right.

These rules are applicable to every person breathing on this planet rich or poor. It calls for us to rethink what we value. Robert's Rules of Economics is about solutions driven by fairness and equality.

Robert's Rules of Optimal Societal Fairness (Rule #1):

"To be socially responsible or not to be socially responsible," that is the question and the answer.

What is societal fairness?

I have defined it to be the following:

When the private sectors, public sectors, and the upper and middle class of a society hold up the living standards of the entire society and share equally the tax responsibilities/burden of caring for the children, the elderly, the poor, and the mentally ill. Our American capitalists must share the cost of our infrastructure, national defense, national debt, natural disasters, and war(s). Our entire society needs to be a part of something that is greater than ourselves.

Free Trade (Rule #2)

Since the eighteenth century, Americans have led the world in all measures and amounts of free trading. Americans have never needed any incentives to free trade with others around the world. We are still the leader in free trading, because every entrepreneur on the planet wants to be in the US markets, the largest and most influential throughout the world. Equilibrium economics is the best vehicle to allow unrestricted free trading to occur. Equilibrium economics is like an invisible hand that controls market transactions with incredible fairness for the entrepreneurs they represent. Many economists felt as I do, that there was never a need for NAFTA or anything like the TPP. It places restrictions on the market and favors wealthy entrepreneurs seeking to create monopolies that limit competition. Tariffs are another huge obstruction to free trading, by causing wars and isolation. Equilibrium economics kicks into high gear with an abundance of competition, not less. Bartering is still the best type of trading and trickle-down is the worst.

Equilibrium Economics (Rule #3)

Economic and Societal Fairness for the Rich and the Poor

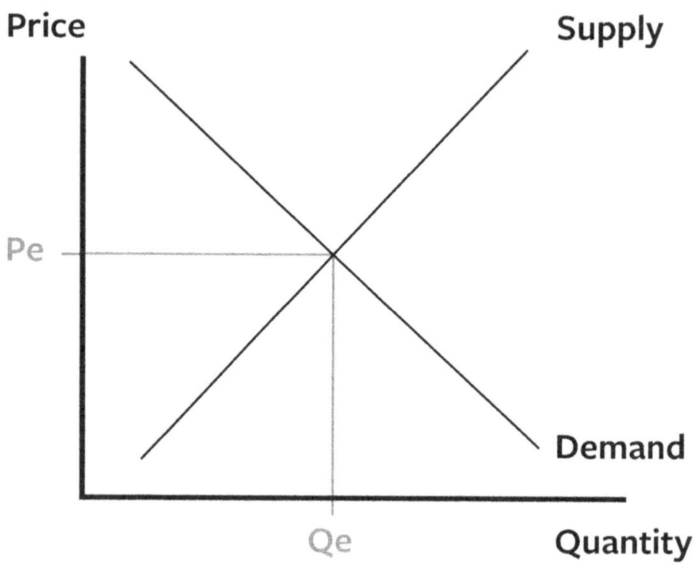

PART ONE

Trickle-Down Economics

Trickle-down economics creates artificial changes in consumer demand curves for goods and services that cannot be sustained to meet monopoly driven supply curves, seeking only to maximize corporate profits. Trickle-down suppresses the salaries and incomes of Americans, of the lower and middle classes, and at the same time forces them to bear the cost of paying the majority of the tax burden. As wealthy Americans create loopholes and reduce their tax liabilities, lower and middle-class Americans have no say as to how or what their tax dollars are spent on. There are plenty of incentives for the wealthy 2 percent to push a minimum life existence on the masses. They get large tax-cuts, creating a large amount of debt that can only be paid by future generations of lower and middle-class workers.

Supply-Siders

Supply-side economics is a macroeconomic theory that argues that reducing taxes on businesses and the wealthy in society is the best way to stimulate business investments and create jobs. According to supply-side economics, consumers will then benefit from a greater supply of goods and services at lower prices, and employment will increase. It is a macroeconomic theory already proven to be full of fallacies.

It was started by economist Robert Mundell and Arthur Laffer during the Ronald Reagan administration. Mundell and Laffer developed the never-proven, fallacious, Laffer curve and trickle-down theories to give large tax cuts to the wealthy: republicans and democrats. Instantly, Ronald Reagan became the Beloved president to all wealthy republicans and democrats. Ronald Reagan became the "Great White Hope" that everybody loved as Nancy Reagan called all the shots. It is a form of laissez-faire capitalism in which transactions between private parties are free from government intervention. The phrase laissez-faire is part of a larger French phrase and basically translates to "let (it/them) do," or to "let go."

Most economists prefer the term "trickle-down economics." These are economic policies which clearly favor the wealthy, while being framed and publicized as something good for the average citizen (lies). By the time any form of prosperity reaches the average citizen, there's nothing left but "toxic wastewater" being trickled-down on our middle class and poor citizens.

I grew up on the theories proposed by economist John Maynard Keynes (1883–1946) referred to as Keynesian economics, in which economic growth is enhanced when the government lowers taxes on the middle class and increases government spending. It's also known as the trickle-up effect or fountain effect, an economic theory used to describe the overall ability of middle-class people to boost the productivity of the economy as a whole, not just wealthy citizens.

"Trickle-down economics has done a great job of creating monopolies and oligopolies. We have a few banks, oil companies, energy providers, farms, and decisionmakers, which are only benefiting "the few." Mr. President, there's just a few too many barriers to entry (prisons), too much collusion (racism/discrimination), too little competition (jobs) for Black citizens to earn humane respect." (Sept. 6, 2016, letter to President Obama)

The Fallacies of Robert Mundell and Arthur Laffer (Curve):

Canadian economist Robert Mundell and American economist Arthur Laffer did not get a Nobel Prize for the Laffer curve and implementing trickle-down budgets. The director of the Office of Management and Budget (1981–1985) under President Ronald Reagan, David Alan Stockman, implemented trickle-down in federal and state budgets for the first time. Mr. Stockman knew when he implemented trickle-down that it would have devastating effects on our economy but he did the party line thing and implemented it anyway. Mr. Stockman should be leading the way back to equilibrium economy and stop complaining about the economic abuses of the day. In support of Stockman's trickle-down economist Robert Mundell, a Canadian, pushed a short-term solution for stagnation that occurred during the 1980s, and it turned into a new movement called supply-side economics. Mundell received the Nobel Memorial Prize in Economic Sciences in 1999 for his work in monetary dynamics and optimum currency areas. A theory looking at geographical regions to maximize economic efficiency and having an entire region sharing a single currency (the Euro).

If Mr. Mundell used trickle-down as a premise in his 1999 work, it should be reexamined. Mr. Mundell's theories put the Europeans on a dangerous, reckless, and unsustainable path using his and Mundell's macro-theories of supply-side economics. Mr. Mundell's economic theories are fallacious and self-serving.

Laissez-faire is good involving private transactions with other private companies, but laissez-faire does not apply when private monies are mixed with government monies.

The Laffer curve makes fallacious assumptions when it assumes that the wealthy will not participate in building an economy when being taxed too heavily. If you tax the wealthy, the wealthy will pass on taxes to those that are buying their products or services.

The Laffer curve only applies to the poorest people on the planet. When you tax them too much, those individuals have nothing to begin with and will be less likely to continue working or pay taxes.

So the rich will continue to take all the tax cuts and breaks they can get. They also have excellent lawyers creating loopholes to hide their wealth. The wealthy continue to make their money off the backs of the middle class and the poor, and feel no obligation to pay higher taxes as part of their American social responsibility.

The Extreme Focus

Trickle-down/supply-side economics has an extreme focus on the supply curves. It gives the wealthy an excuse to not pay their fair share of taxes, and an altered tax system (full of loopholes). Supply curves are price schedules that show the various amounts of a product the wealthy are willing to produce and make available for consumers rich and poor. The wealthy will offer more of a product to consumers as prices go up, but will offer smaller amounts of the products to consumers as prices go down. Trickle-down is very insensitive to the needs of the lower /middle-class consumer. The consumer demands for products are quite the opposite and rely on having disposable incomes

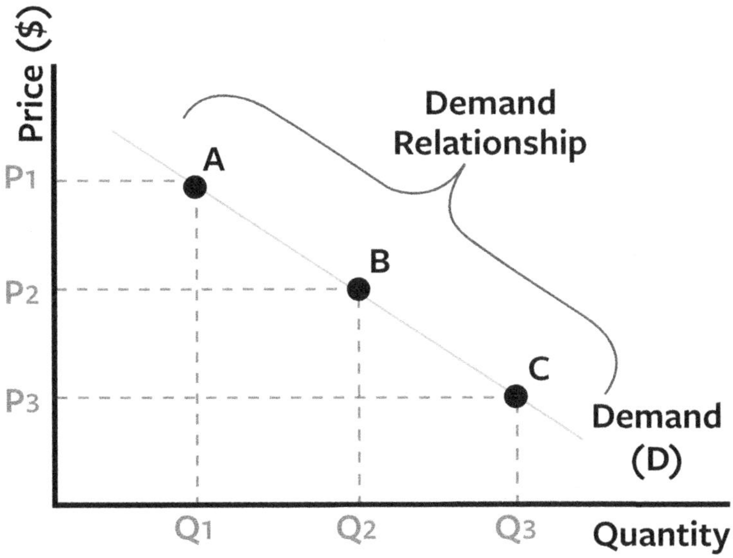

The lower the price, the more consumers can afford to buy.

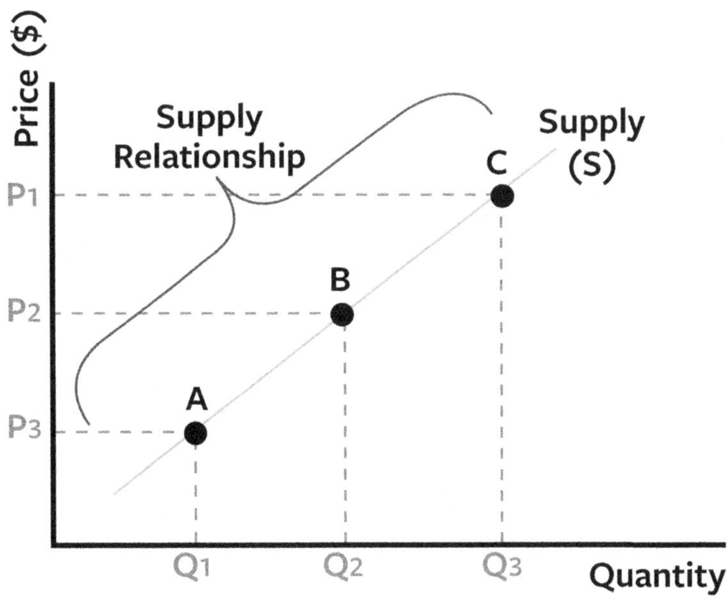

The higher the price, the more producers are willing to supply.

to buy products. So when prices go down, lower/middle-class consumers are willing and able to buy more of what they need or want.

Ronald Reagan/Paul Ryan Protecting the Wealthy:

Ronald Reagan was not an economist and was given bad advice that he successfully sold to US citizens and the world. Most Americans knew Nancy and Ronald Reagan loved this country but they put all Americans on a dangerous economic path to self-destruction and ruin. Misguided, Congressman Paul Ryan is in the swamp selling trickle-down like never before.

I was majoring in economics at the time of the Reagan roll out of the new term "supply-side economics," a term never used or mentioned in any of the economics classes I took at the University of Washington. At the time, few economists knew the dangers or complexities of supply-side economics so it was just called "Reaganomics." As soon as rational economists began looking at Reaganomics closely, other new terrifying terms came out to describe it: trickle-down economics, free-market economics (not fair market), and voodoo economics. That was the beginning of the rigged system for the richest 2 percent of Americans.

Paul Harvey, a conservative American radio broadcaster for ABC, is credited with popularizing the terms "Reaganomics" and "guesstimate" and he was not even an economist. That's like trying to develop policies set by Rush Limbaugh (sickening and skewed views). And now you know the rest of the story: misguided Congressman Paul Ryan is currently promoting trickle-down policies for the wealthiest 2 percent.

Republican economic policies have taken human fairness

out of every equation regarding social responsibilities by cutting funding that supports the growth of human capital (the everyday worker). They will not fund projects or endeavors that improve the lives of everyday people without large, guaranteed profits for themselves. They only propose trickle-down budgets full of loopholes that protect the wealthiest Americans, since trickle-down policies take from the poor middle-class and give to the rich.

Equilibrium Economic Analysis (Rule #4)

Spineless Republican Congressman Paul Ryan received a letter from me after proposing the continuation of another set of trickle-down policies in 2014. Trickle-down policies are the only policies Paul Ryan and his daddy ever mastered and he knows nothing else.

"It is my opinion, we need both Congressman Ryan, human and financial capital to make our economy work, why do you continue cutting off growth in human capital? Your goal should be trying to get our economy as close to full employment and full production as possible. The failed trickle-down ideologies failed because it only addressed growth in financial capital markets, very old news. Whatever you do to one side of the equation you must do to the other side in order to maintain market equilibrium. It's just a little macroeconomics and basic math Congressman." (September 15, 2014 letter to US Congressman Paul Ryan)

It is extremely important to always know where equilibrium is in the market and what reasons you would allow the markets to be temporarily out of equilibrium.

Trickle-down economics has our economy running fast and hot—white hot. What our economy needs most is to cool down to a rate that is sustainable. People are crying out for fairness and equal treatment, and equilibrium economics is the solution. Equilibrium economics is a better economic approach to managing a capitalist society that includes fairness and a level playing field for all. It is a system that is responsible and has integrity when dealing with our obligations toward social responsibilities (being good citizens).

A trickle-down driven economy is kind of like driving a car really fast in third gear and third gear only. Equilibrium economics allows the economy to shift into fourth gear (or sustainability) and offers the possibility of true economic growth for both the rich and poor middle class when shifted into fifth gear. There is no need to burn through the world's resources, create global warming, and run our economy at a rate that is unsustainable.

We need to stop, take a deep breath, and get back to the basics of capitalism and how to manage a capitalistic society back into equilibrium. The United States should be taking a leadership role in getting back to the basics of managing capitalist markets through the use of equilibrium economic analysis (EEA). Equilibrium economics will require the capitalist to recognize both the supply and demand curves.

Economics professors around the world should switch the order of their terminology and focus from "supply and demand" to "demand and supply." Our future entrepreneurs and economists need to focus first on the demand curves for production efficiencies to reduce financial and human waste, not supply curves. We need to have a demand-driven society to become better stewards of our people and our environment.

"The most efficient and humane way for capitalist markets to operate is in equilibrium."

Equilibrium in a capitalist market is too important not to know where it lies, which is our current situation. A healthy

Profit Maximation - the MR=MC Approach
Profit-maximizing case

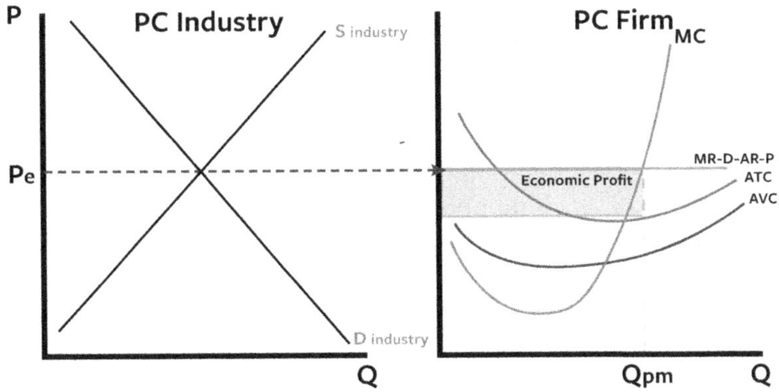

analysis of a capitalist society starts with knowing where the equilibrium point is in the market. Then and only then, will economists be able to examine the short and long-term effects of operating capitalist markets above or below equilibrium (surpluses and shortages). This is not new economics and has been taught in major universities around the world.

The point where both supply and demand curves intersect is known as the equilibrium point. Equilibrium means "in balance" or "at rest." No complaints from producers or consumers. The equilibrium point is the most critical point in managing healthy markets. Supply-side theorists are all about the supply curves and ignoring consumer demand curves entirely, resulting in extreme polarization and confusion. Trickle-down/supply-siders are polarizing our markets, our politics, and our religious beliefs. Equilibrium economics provides competition in the marketplace and that allows the rich and the poor opportunities to acquire economic profits.

Disequilibrium, polarization, Monopolies and Oligopolies

With private monopolies and oligopolies in play, the rich capitalist has the ability to restrict entry to the market and persistently enjoy "economic profits" when demand is strong.

The effect of operating markets long term in disequilibrium is the cause of extreme polarization between the rich and the middle class/poor. Long-term market disequilibrium creates the right conditions for monopolies and oligopolies to flourish.

A monopoly exists when a single firm is the sole producer of a product for which there are no close substitutes. There is an absence of competition that characterizes a monopoly.

The basic characteristic of oligopoly is "fewness." Oligopoly exists whenever a few firms dominate the market for a product. When we hear of the "Big Three," "Big Four," or "Big Six," we can be relatively certain that the industry is oligopolistic. The dominant few may control 70 or 80 percent of the market.

Oligopoly banks like Wells Fargo need to be broken up to protect consumers because they are too big and still can't seem to do anything right, but have been in business since the mid-1800s. They can create phony accounts using your name to make money and somehow lose all your personal information to cyber thieves looking to steal your identity. Wells Fargo cannot be trusted and flaunts its authority over the everyday unprotected citizen.

I created the chart on the next page to depict monopoly profits. I believe that monopoly companies are able and willing to bend back the supply curve and wipe out their closest competition. In doing so, they're able to create monopoly profits above and beyond economic profits in a competitive industry. Monopoly profits are becoming the new norm. Monopoly firms

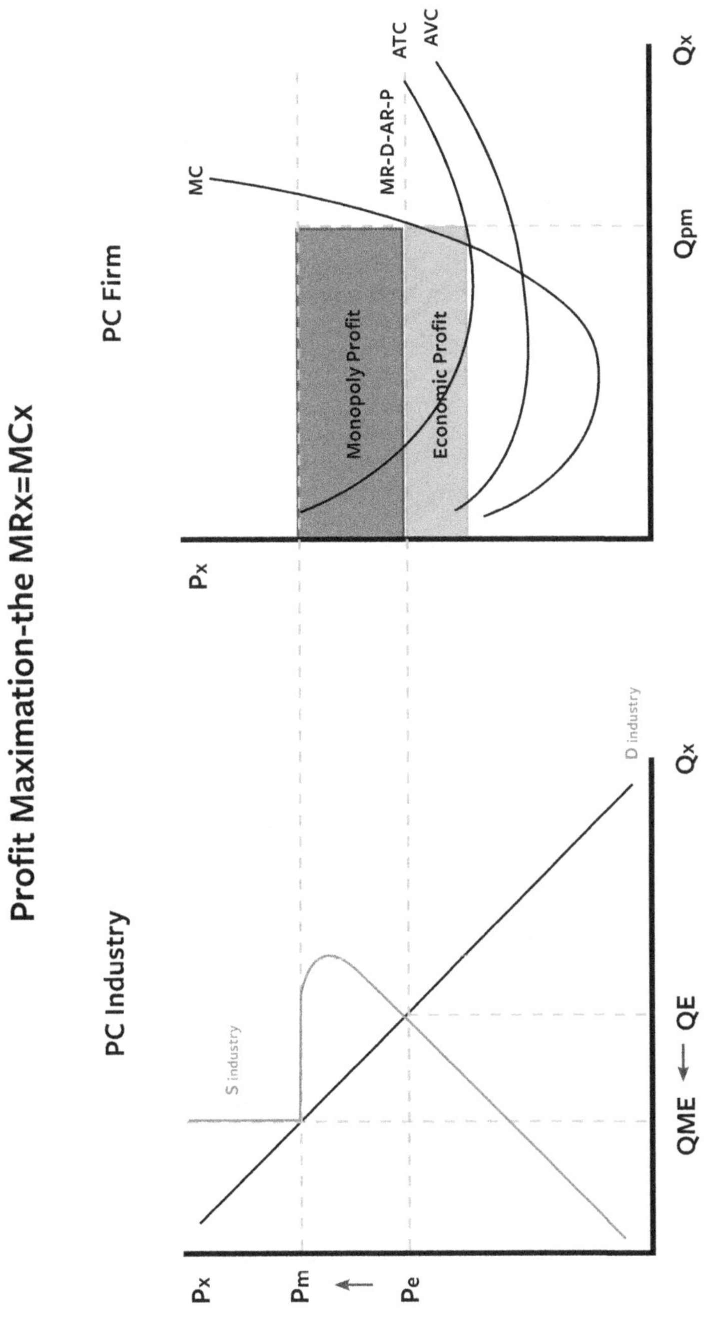
Profit Maximation-the MRx=MCx
PC Industry
PC Firm
Px
Pm
Pe
S industry
D industry
QME
QE
Qx
Px
MC
MR-D-AR-P
ATC
AVC
Monopoly Profit
Economic Profit
Qpm
Qx

are able to set prices to be whatever they choose. The everyday consumer will pick up the cost, as the increases take a higher percentage of their monthly disposable incomes, while at the same time small and midsize entrepreneurs lose their investment capital and businesses. The monopoly company will consider it as the cost of doing business and just pass on the cost to the consumers.

This monopolistic behavior is unfair to small startups and midsize businesses trying to create a niche ("fair competition") for themselves and lower prices for consumers.

Prolonged use of supply-side economics has skewed and rigged the markets in favor of monopolies and monopolistic behavior. This allows heartless, cowardly entrepreneurs like Donald Trump to be a force to be reckoned with. Some of the current monopolistic companies taking competition out of our marketplace are: mainstream media, newspapers, banking, Pfizer, NRA, Google, Amazon, Walmart, Facebook, the pharmaceutical industry, oil, automotive, big tobacco and large brewing companies vs craft beers, just to name a few. Who will decide how much control is too much control over consumers?

We need a government that will implement equilibrium economic policies to provide the checks and balances needed in the public and private sectors of our market economy and help in the development of a more perfect union.

Capitalism is extreme when...

- Capitalist are allowed to create large inequalities in income, wealth and opportunities.
- Competition is allowed to go unchecked.
- The middle class starts to fade away and become part of the new poor.

- Consensus on how and what is to be done to solve social problems cannot be reached.
- Capitalists can exploit labor contracts to create wage slavery, by keeping their employees at a minimum wage instead of providing a living wage.
- Capitalists are allowed to created monopolies and oligopolies that are restricting true market competition.
- When capitalists are allowed to weaken or have no antitrust laws that protect consumers.
- Capitalists are allowed to develop a pattern of receiving large permanent tax cuts while small temporary tax cuts are provided for the poor and middle class.
- A few capitalists are allowed to control the lives of the masses.
- Capitalists excessively use nondisclosure agreements to conceal wrongdoing.
- Capitalist are allowed to hire gatekeepers and enablers to blatantly tell lies to the public for profit.
- Airline capitalists are allowed to fix prices.
- Capitalist employers can screen out those looking for work, based strictly on the color of their skin.
- Public utility capitalists are allowed to raise prices for electricity, gas, water, and coal for monopoly profits.
- Legal capitalists are allowed to charge large legal fees for minor offenses.
- High medical expenses force families into bankruptcy, and citizens neglect their own health.
- Capitalists are allowed silly notions of one currency, one world.
- Capitalists are allowed to not pay taxes and neglect their social responsibilities.
- Congress and the supreme courts gives up our liberties to a president without checks and balances.

- Government capitalists use trickle-down as a quick fix to throw millions of Americans off of their health care.
- Capitalists are able to convince the Supreme Court that Citizens United is the best way to protect our democracy and the concept of "one man, one vote."
- Capitalists are allowed to ignore basic human rights for profit.
- The national debt becomes the burden of our great grand babies.
- Capitalists are not given the right incentives to reinvest in America, like in our infrastructure.
- The benefits and the requirements for citizenship are not equal.
- Sex offenders seek relief from the Catholic Church, politicians, and the criminal justice system.

The more extreme capitalism becomes, the stronger the tendency for a society to move closer to socialism/populism in search of a quick fix and some economic fairness. Just look at the popularity of Bernie Sanders during the 2016 election. His message of quick-fix fairness became overshadowed by his anger and public mistrust of Ms. Clinton, leading to a Trump victory.

Bernie Sanders and his supporters divided the Democratic Party with his independent-style campaign of "political revolution" politics. Just like the Tea Party ruined the Republican Party. Bernie Sanders and his supporters divided the Democratic Party resulting in compromised Putin/Trump voters or non-voters. A shadow man that was never a democrat, not then and not now.

"If you were a true democrat you would have known how important the 2017 election was, and you would have been a part of a one-two punch to knocking out Donald Trump. Instead you and most of your supporters became independent obstructionists." (September 29, 2017, letter to Senator Bernard Sanders)

Historically Extremely/Skewed Policies

White, wealthy Americans have historically established extreme/skewed policies when they felt afraid or threatened and looked for ways to protect their individual wealth. The legal formation of slavery was one of the first extreme policies imposed on Black people.

Trickle-down is just another form of these extreme policies being imposed on non-wealthy people. Black Americans and Native Americans have experienced legally protected bigotry since the beginning of the "American Dream."

During and after World War II, ask our Japanese Americans how they were treated. After the sixties' civil rights revolution, policies were put in place to lock up Black and Brown citizens. Now after 9/11, the invasion of Iraq, and the creation of an Islamic State, do you think American Muslim communities have anything to worry about? Muslim Americans are facing some new harsh restrictions. Donald Trump, one of the most polarizing and extreme presidents in American history, is attempting to restrict the mobility of Muslim Americans, instead of trying to help those communities find solutions.

Trickle-down economic theory has been a terrible experiment in modernizing capitalism, in favor of the very wealthy and modern entrepreneurs who are restricting competition in the market place to protect their wealth.

When the markets are guided by the forces of equilibrium, the macroeconomic markets within a capitalist society can function very well in handling the problems facing a modern society. When markets are out of equilibrium for long periods of time, the ability to make corrections quickly decreases. Our economy begins to look like our largest cargo ship making a 90-degree turn in the ocean. It just cannot respond quickly, if at all.

Trickle-down macroeconomic theory skews our markets out of equilibrium. Trickle-down policies function as a mechanism to cause large inequalities between those who have and those who have not. Trickle-down leftovers are all that is offered to the other 98 percent of Americans, while huge unspeakable profits are funneling-up to the wealthy 2 percent of Americans. A fair return on investments should be the goal, not seeking extreme slightly taxed profits.

In Colorado, the republicans/conservative/libertarians have implemented "TABOR" to protect the wealthy in Colorado from paying their fair share of taxes. TABOR stands for "The Taxpayer Bill of Rights" and those Colorado citizens that are poor or middle class or under-represented do not have a voice or a seat at the table, in this skewed form of so-called "Bill of Rights." It is not a charter of Colorado citizens' rights, but a provision requiring that increases in the overall State tax revenue be tied to inflation and population increases unless larger increases are approved by a direct vote by the entire electorate. These are only "rights" for the rich in Colorado, disguising the trickle-down results that tax the middle class and poor without meeting their basic needs.

As a result, there is never enough state tax revenue for the basics such as, to pays for Colorado schools, healthcare, daycare, infrastructure projects (roads, dams, bridges, light rail, bullet trains connecting the coast), and environmental issues. Revenue should be available and is needed to keep Colorado competitive and contributing to the US gross domestic product. The wealthy have chosen to pocket the money rather than reinvest in our connected future, resulting in lost opportunities, huge deficits, and deferred maintenance cost to pass on to our kids and grandkids to pay for. The Taxpayers Bill of Rights in Colorado is all about ownership not partnership. It has never been about "Life liberty and the pursuit of happiness," but more about "life liberty and the pursuit of profits."

Repetitive Mistakes

Economic theories/policies have been able to prevail for centuries and decades. It can happen when a few wealthy dictators, nations/kingdoms come together and agree to try and control everything and everybody through the use of skewed economic policies.

Our institutions have to have safeguards in place with rational/ethical citizens in our three branches of government and strong antitrust laws to keep the greed of mankind from destroying itself with money as the only incentive to motivate people.

In one form or another, George H. W. Bush, Bill Clinton, George W. Bush, and Donald Trump continued to use a skewed tax system full of loopholes to protect the wealthy through the use and abuse of trickle-down economic policies, taking from the poor and giving to the rich. Robin Hood in reverse.

The Reagan Attraction (Greed)

Ronald Reagan, was a very popular movie-star president. He stuck to the lines he was given about trickle-down and said it with a lot of compassion.

He forgot to mention, or was unaware, that trickle-down economic policies in the short term would get republicans and democrats off his back, but had no idea how hard trickle-down would be to stop, or how divisive and polarizing the policies could be in the long term. Ronald and Nancy Reagan loved this country and would have never implemented these destructive policies if they would have known the long-term implications.

Trickle-down economics did not expand prosperity to all American workers. It has only expanded the prosperity of the wealthiest 2 percent of the US population.

The trickle-down American capitalists earned their wealth and fortune by exploiting American labor and now want to be free of fair US taxation and choose not to pay pension benefits to senior workers. These greedy Americans are now ready to exploit labor worldwide and hide their profits offshore. Who cares about the gap between rich and poor? We all know it's not the rich.

Rich American capitalists are able to live free, arrogant, and proud of their untouchable wealth. The American trickle-down capitalists have foolishly convinced themselves that it's okay to pee ("trickle-down") on American laborers and go to other countries without any social obligations. These foolish, short-term-thinking capitalist Americans have also convinced themselves that they don't need the manufacturing help of American laborers, one of the best labor markets for manufacturing on the planet, if they would only bring it back to America. It's okay to "trickle-down" on American labor by paying minimum wages, while owners/capitalists take home excessive profits and golden parachutes to move on. The trickle-down capitalist is greedy and self-centered; constantly looking for new ways to exploit cheap labor and resources to gather their unforeseen profits.

As the risk and the cost of doing business in other countries continue to rise, the trickle-down capitalist will come running back to the safety of the US borders and labor market

Iniside & Outside the Production Possibilities

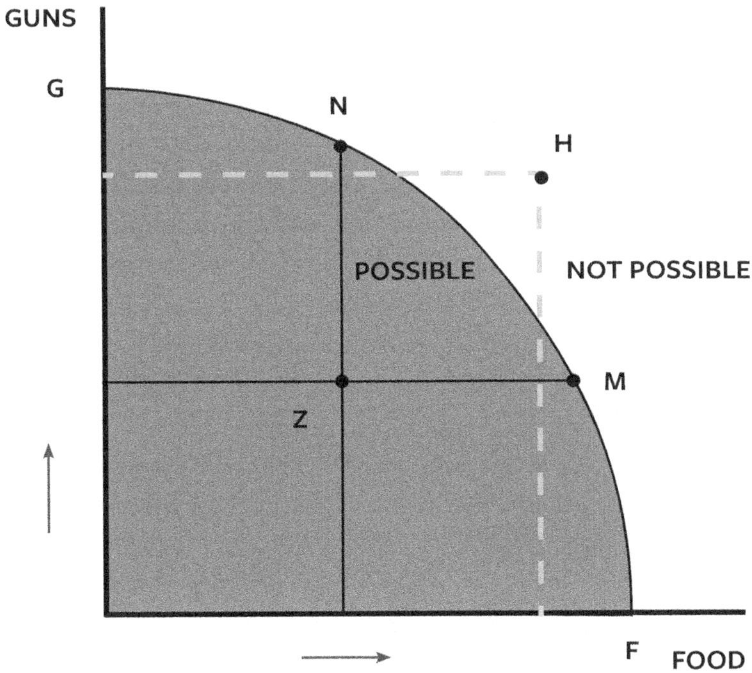

place—if it's not totally destroyed by long-term trickle-down budgets that are implemented at home. We have to remember that trickle-down policies and budgets are a rigged system for the wealthy.

Twenty-plus years of Reaganomics has caused our economy to be in disequilibrium. Ronald Reagan and what he foresaw for America and American workers almost came true. Reagan said that Americans could not, and would not, produce anything in America anymore and that we were going to become a low paid, service industry-based economy like China and Japan. All Reagan envisioned was Americans providing services to others.

Taking American production and manufacturing out of the country to exploit other around the world. Trickle-down is the real redistribution of wealth, and it only serves the needs of the wealthy.

If a country could put all of its resources (land, labor, capital and entrepreneurship) together to produce two and only two products (guns or food) the society could now decide which products it needed or wanted most produced to meet the needs of the society. In times of war, we would need more guns and at times of peace more food. Only the combinations on the ark between "G" and "F" are the most efficient possible choices for the society to produce. Any production inside the ark "G" and "F" is not using resources in the most efficient or effective manner.

If the society is at a point like "Z" inside the ark, is a red flag for an economist like me. It indicates the society's tax dollars are being wasted by lack of competition, or inefficient use of resources. The society is plagued with all types of labor issues related to race, sex, age, gender, and the disabled citizens facing production discrimination in the workplace.

If the society is able to solve most of the problems created by point "Z" (unequal treatment of human and natural resources) and wanted to produce more food during peaceful times, or at war increase the production of guns and move away from point "Z" to points somewhere between points "M" and "N."

Point "H" is outside the production possibility curve for both the production of guns and food, and the society is unable to achieve "H."

The Power of the 2 percent Market Owners

For the wealthy 2 percent of Americans, the concept of budget fairness is gone. You know if you cut from one side of the equation... you cut from the other side of the equation (simple math). Reasonable profit fairness is also gone because the 2 percent want to maximize profits at the expense of the labor force.

Trickle-down allows the market owners to decide the value of everything and everybody—what will be produced, how much will be produced, when it will be produced, by whom it will be produced, how much it will cost and how much, and who will be paid. However, more than just supply and demand for goods and services, skewed markets also make it more difficult to address social problems. The economy will function at its best when the markets are in equilibrium, for those with wealth as well as for those trying to acquire wealth. Equilibrium markets work for all Americans.

So what you have now are wealthy market owners that are Republicans, Democrats, and Independent voters profiting by trickle-down economic theories and that is why it is so hard to stop, even though trickle-down is ripping our country apart. In the long-run, many small business owners will be driven out of the market due to lack of financial resources and competition.

Those receiving the large tax cuts should be asked to finance health care for every American and a larger portion of our defense spending, as it is the multinational corporations that are more likely to get our country into a war seeking to maximize profits worldwide.

PART TWO

Robert's Realities

Thank You President Obama

The worst of Reagan's vision for America would have come true if it were not for President Obama. President Obama saved the banking and auto industries and created a shift from trickle-down economics to middle-class economics. President Obama was smart enough to stimulate the return of manufacturing in America. Common-sense economics is growing the middle class and giving the right incentives to the manufacturing industries to stay and grow in America. You ask, "What is common sense economics?" "It is when macro and micro economic market analyses begin and end with knowing where equilibrium is in the market." It's okay to be out of equilibrium for short periods of time, but knowing how to get back in equilibrium will be the challenge.

Political Economist and the Religious Economist

"Your Holiness, the world needs you and your messages more than ever, and God does not give us more than we can handle. The world needs to be reminded that the first economists were theologians, and when Your Holiness, speaks out against "unfettered capitalism," our world leaders should understand there is precedence for you doing so, on both biblical and secular terms." (February 20, 2014, letter to Your Holiness)

Wake up! Like it or not, it's economic know how that runs the two most powerful human organizations on the planet, the political economist and the religious economist. Religious economic theory and political economic theory...what other disciplines are there, that attempt to control the daily behavior of men and women on this planet? We need both of these macro markets to be in equilibrium for world peace. Both markets have been known to be brutal on society and at times inhumane. What's in the cards for the twenty-first century? Are we going to be brutal toward one another? Or are we going to be more peaceful and humane toward one another? Do we want our economics to favor one group over another or do we want our economy to be on a level playing field?

Black Economics (Rule #5)

I grew up (1950s and '60s) during the time when Black Americans (the Black Panthers) were taking control of their own destiny and that made white America fearful and over-reactionary. I grew up during the time when President Kennedy was assassinated, Martin Luther King was assassinated, and Bobby Kennedy was assassinated, when Malcolm X and the Black Panthers were destroyed. I grew up when there was little or no trust by the Black community in our government. Americans were trying to recover from the Vietnam War and Richard Nixon added to an already distrusted government. Black people in America had very few leaders to reach out to.

After the sixties' civil rights revolution, White, privileged, racist America began to overreact to the Black movements and went back to rigging the courts, elections, and the justice system, resulting in police murders and mass Black incarceration. Mandatory sentences for nonviolent crimes became one of the contrived processes for locking up large numbers of Black and Brown people. White politicians started putting Black people away for long periods of time for small amounts of marijuana and crack while White folks got a slap on the hand for snorting large amounts of powdered cocaine.

My own personal professional working career was obstructed by constant unfounded attacks by White males and females. Working in the aerospace industry in the eighties, Blacks represented less than 1 percent of the workforce. I was an easy target for the haters to come after especially after forming the first Black Employees Association of Lockheed Martin workers or "BEST" (Black Employee Support Team).

I was successful in the workplace by giving my ideas away and letting the White boys take all the credit. If it could be identified that the idea came from me it was a bad idea. It was ultimately the racist tasteless jokes about Black babies being stuck on the wall with their lips, that I would not laugh at, being wrongfully accused of stalking, being compared to chimpanzees and forced to sign (2) non-disclosure agreements that finally moved me out of the workplace at age fifty-seven (when I should have been making the most money of my professional career).

Is mass incarceration of Black and Brown in America an accident, or was it by design? To this day, America has more of their own citizens locked up than any other country in the world. Black Americans have been looking for leadership on the subject, hoping to resolve mass incarceration of young Black males for many years without success. It's only recently that White Americans have acknowledged the problem. With cameras in the hands of every person on the street being put on police, a wake-up call has occurred—a call for help. At the federal level, only President Obama and Attorney General Eric Holder and Loretta Lynch focused Americans on resolving this enormous American human tragedy. National health care, middle-class economics, Black Lives Matter, and Black think tanks might finally give Black Americans some relief. I wrote "Roberts Letters" mostly during the time President Obama was in office. They are food-for-thought letters written by me to people that may not be in touch with reality or people I deeply admire. The letters were written to be my way of making a small difference.

White Privilege

Donald Trump, "You know what I am? I'm a Nationalist"
By Peter Baker, *The New York Times*, Wednesday October 24, 2018

Donald Trump and Putin have the privilege to hate President Obama and I believe they worked together on the birther campaign against President Obama. Trump colluded with Putin to hurt our president and attack our democracy.

America harbors many individuals seeking to hold onto white privilege and racist policies and they won't apologize for it. Talk to Donald Trump about making any apologies for his hateful rhetoric. Guys like the Koch brothers (buying elections) and Donald Trump, will go on abusing their White privileges if not forced to stop.

Republicans proudly call themselves "the Party of Opposition," as House Speaker Paul Ryan did in December of 2015. Most of them are cowards, White boys unable to keep White boys accountable. Republicans in Congress ignored repeated requests from President Obama to implement tougher gun laws in an effort to protect Americans against domestic terror without success. The result is a bunch of mostly White males who think this country has been taken away from them by Black and Brown Americans. We see politicians with hateful rhetoric leading ignorant members of our population with the resources they need to conduct cowardly acts of domestic terror and violence unchecked. This has resulted in a huge spike in recent years in gun attacks. The republicans and the NRA are without doubt holding Americans hostage at gunpoint to sell whatever to whomever they want. Most Americans know that semiautomatic weapons and assault rifles are used only for hunting people, not deer, not moose, not rabbits or squirrels. "Just irresponsible ignorant White boys."

When republicans talk about the social net, they only talk about food stamps, housing, and welfare programs, programs paid for by tax dollars; they never say anything about the employees at NASA and the defense industries that have large salaries and bonuses and great retirements and pay no taxes.

The concepts of privatization are an effort by the wealthy to steal taxpayer money and render services to those that can afford it only, wealthy politicians, and the rich and famous. Reducing the services to the poor (cost cutting) and making services too costly for the poor to engage in any part of the American dream.

Republicans want to privatize health care to make it affordable to them and the rich, with no concern for middle or low income Americans. Healthcare in America should not operate strictly for profit (our current direction), but should be for every American like it is in other industrialized countries that value their citizens. A healthy workforce is a more productive workforce. After all, American citizens deserve to have the best healthcare possible. Dentistry is an industry that needs to be regulated and part of our health care. Supply-siders in our society are like leeches and ticks ready to suck the blood and money out of any marketplace for personal gain.

Republicans should not lie to Americans about repealing and replacing healthcare without having a better option. But Republicans will tell you, "It's not against the law nor a crime to lie to the public."

Pharmaceutical companies have become oligopolies. They should not be able to charge American consumers prices that are above their equilibrium point and ignore demand curves. Charging Americans prices above the equilibrium point is a current pharmaceutical practice and is a function of trickle-down greed. The effects of trickle-down have been devastating to American health and our economy. The drug industries just want to get rich. They don't care if they get citizens addicted or killed, as long as they get paid. Take as much as you can, for as long as you can.

Donald Trump appears to be the leader of the radical, ignorant, cowardly groups of Aryan Nation and clan members of American society that plot and kill just like other terrorist groups around the world. Mr. Trump's hateful rhetoric is rallying his supporters to go after Muslim Americans. It is clear that we are being led by one of America's most uneducated, privileged, wealthy fool, and his friends. President Trump pulled the United States out of the Paris climate accord because he is uneducated. The world knows the truth about climate change.

It should be illegal for leaders of the free world to profess hatred in public. With the number of mentally ill individuals in the world, it only invites them to act out hateful against others. Those that profess hate toward others are not leaders.

How cowardly of President Donald Trump to impose policies that would separate babies from their parents in the name of border security. There is no compassion in this policy for parents or babies, it's arrogant, hateful, ignorant, and not representative of who we want to be as Americans.

Another sad features of White privilege are the treatment of all women as property. Women have socially benefited the most since affirmative action and maybe now they're finally asserting one of their rights, not to be sexually assaulted in the workplace. Let's be clear what this is. These are men forcing themselves on women and some men. These are the same men that are fighting against equal pay for equal work.

White privilege is when White males are allowed to shoot up Black churches and Jewish synagogues and only gets charged with a hate crime instead of domestic violence charges when clearly these are acts of domestic violence as well. If these kind of shooting were conducted by a Black or Brown person it would include domestic violence charges. Another form of pure White privilege.

As for Donald Trump, I agree with former President Jimmy Carter's comments on Friday June 28, 2019, at a Carter Center Event at a resort in Leesburg, Virginia. "Jimmy Carter says he sees Trump as an illegitimate president."

White, rich men and women are not losing their rights, they are simply being asked to share their rights with other Americans; and that might be asking too much.

Demeaning President Obama

The South African government treated Nelson Mandela better than Republicans treated President Obama. The new Republican Grand Old Party (GOP) has chosen its new leader and its Donald J. Trump even if the devil and Putin helped to get him elected. For all we know, Donald Trump could be considering pardoning Putin for the Russian interference in our elections.

Angry White boys and girls feel like they've suffered for eight years during the Obama administration and now they will have a Grand Old Party that would include hanging Black people in public as they eat and listen to music, if they could silence the press. "Repeal and replace" lies how many votes? How do we mitigate hatred? Somehow we have to challenge haters to challenge themselves, and not live a hateful life. Our leaders should make it illegal to publicly profess hatred toward a group or a person.

Overshadowing all of the US efforts to fight terrorism in America and around the world, we have the Edward Snowden effect... we have not forgotten that traitor who flipped right after Obama was elected. The traitor who disclosed how we gather and collect intelligence information.

During times of war, historically Americans rally behind their president in support for their leadership. Instead, republicans disrespected and belittled President Obama by calling him a liar and made it very difficult to show united leadership during war. Republicans were blatantly unprofessional during the whole Obama administration. Republican senators were publicly arrogant, saying they didn't respect the president, they didn't listen to the president and they didn't want the president to be successful.

What is acceptable or unacceptable behavior when you have White privilege and a Black president? Unprofessionalism and racism starts to look the same to the Black professional after a passage of time. There is a fine line between nonprofessionalism and racism, and republican senators used both to demean and belittle Obama and the office of the president. The no, no, hell no, strategy was both. Nonprofessionalism allows for the lies to come and go, when racism is the culprit that divides the United States. Arrogant White professionals have the privilege of being unprofessional and racist if they chose. The nonprofessionalism and racism that took place in the White House for Obama was beyond comprehension for most Americans, White or Black. At some point, even privileged White Americans will have to question their results with President Donald Trump.

Republicans continue to lie about their efforts to reach out to the minority populations when in reality they only wish to serve themselves and their rich donors by expanded White privilege. After President Obama was elected, republicans went into private meetings and swore not to work with this president—to make him a one term president and to say no to everything President Obama tried to propose. Republicans did not care about anything except getting that Black president out. Some republicans called our president a Muslim. Their treatment of President Obama was nothing short of treasonous at times: while addressing Congress, republicans called President Obama a liar. Republicans have called President Obama a Nazi, compared him to Hitler, and called to impeach him without cause. Republicans have done nothing to help move our country forward, only backward, while never offering up any solutions of their own.

Republicans have no shame in their game. They planned to embarrass and belittle President Obama any time they could. Despite the attacks, it was amazing what President Obama was able to accomplish. Privileged White racist paranoia finally started to get addressed in the criminal justice system. For the first time, Americans have major health care reform. Our youth are waking up to racial inequality with the Black Lives Matter campaign. If America is able to stay focused on Obama's middle class economics, our country will finally get away from trickle-down and be on the road to economic equilibrium recovery.

Golden Rules for the Wealthy

What are the golden rules for wealthy American citizens in a capitalistic society? There appears to be only one golden rule for the wealthiest Americans and that is: "What I want on this planet should always override the needs and wants of the majority." Do any other rules really apply to the wealthy? Are our wealthy Americans even thinking about being responsible for the inequities they cause? Are there any proven dos or don'ts for the wealthiest citizens while engaging one another? Is being socially responsible on the list? Or is it just about the individual? Is caring for your fellow citizens, in any way, on the list?

Polarization

Economic, political, and religious polarization is the result of prolonged focus on trickle-down economics. It's polarizing the divide between the rich and the poor in America and around the world. The supply curves have become inelastic and virtually parallel, creating economic polarization for which only the wealthy can afford to produce or buy. Polarization will continue to create more monopolies, oligopolies, and market predators in search of insane and unreasonable profits. Trickle-down economics has created the polarization of our politics and our religion exponentially over the last forty years. You can have it, if you can afford it. White, rich people are not losing their rights they are being asked to share their rights with others. Our future is uncertain.

FY2018 Economic Environmental Leeches & Parasites:

This is a list of leeches and parasites in our society that make up a large part of the swamp. Companies that contribute nothing to our society's welfare, with no idea of what being socially responsible is about, only happy about paying minimum wages, paying no taxes to achieve monopoly profits. Instead of draining the swamp, these companies are being encouraged to cheat at the expense of other Americans. Encouraging capitalist predators to prey on our society without any checks and balances. These companies don't care about human capital nor the environmental responsibilities. I believe in capitalism but we need equilibrium economics to make capitalism work best for the Americans.

This list of companies who were identified in *The New York Times* article, published April 29, 2019, written by Stephanie Saul and Patricia Cohen, titled "Profitable Giants Like Amazon Pay $0 in Corporate Taxes. Some Voters Are Sick of It." The source of the information came from the Institute on Taxation and Economic Policy by Scott Reinhard. Let's be perfectly clear here, these companies are a big part of our economic problem by not contributing taxes to our national defense, our infrastructure, our national disasters and wars. What is even more shameful is they do nothing for the welfare of our children, the elderly, the poor or the mentally ill. Capitalism in itself is not perfect and these companies are clear examples of how it's failing our society. We have to do a better job of draining the swamp. Here is the list of economic environmental swamp dwelling leeches and parasites:

Amazon
Delta Air Lines
Chevron
General Motors
EOG Resources
Duke Energy
Occidental Petroleum
Dominion Energy
Honeywell
Deere & Company
American Electric Power
Public Service Enterprise
Kinder Morgan
Prudential Financial
First Energy
Xcel Energy
PulteGroup
WEC Energy
Molson Coors
Devon Energy
Pioneer Natural Resources
DTE Energy
PPL
Halliburton
Ameren
Netflix
IBM
CMS Energy
Salesforce

The thirty most-profitable, swamp-dwelling companies (leeches and parasites) that paid no federal income taxes in 2018, just sucking the wealth out of our economy.

American Courts

The US Supreme Court is outdated and in need of a major overhaul. These narrow-minded justices need a wake-up call to focus on legally bringing out the best that we represent as Americans. Instead it has turned in to a bipartisan calamity of errors. Since Thurgood Marshall was succeeded by Clarence Thomas, "partisanship" not "statesmanship" has been the order of the republican court. Maybe it's time to add six or more justices to the Supreme Court, since the US population has increased so much.

Apparently Chief Justice John G. Roberts believes Americans are best served by Citizens United v. FEC, which former President Jimmy Carter describes as "dismantling our democracy." The former president goes on to say, "Unlimited political bribery" is the new norm for American politics or, in other words, the "new democracy."

Donald Trump represents the "new democracy" where money and entertainment come together while ethics and morals go out with the bathwater and babies. Where has civility in American politics gone? For republicans, civility is now checked off as just being politically correct. On the highest court in the nation, you will find a sexual predator, cowards, and political cloneys. Chief Justice John G. Roberts is unqualified and an embarrassment to be head of the Supreme Court. Roberts and Thomas are cowards and political cloneys and should be impeached.

The Supreme Court needs to be more diverse, the republicans have already confirmed a sexual predator on the court, so let's pick someone other than the accused Judge Kavanaugh... perhaps a woman. Notorious Ruth Bader Ginsburg is a ray of light and hope for the future.

Cost Benefit Analysis of Trickle-Down Policies:

The concept of giving large permanent tax cuts to the wealthy in our society to solve the world problems is a total structural economic fallacy. In a cost-benefit analysis, the citizen/consumers would have to ask themselves, am I being rational voting to continue trickle-down policies?

If the added benefits of continuing trickle-down policies exceed the cost associated with trickle-down policies, then it is rational to continue those policies.

But is the added cost of continuing trickle-down policies are greater than the added benefits of continuing trickle-down policies is not rational and actions to continue trickle-down policies should not be taken.

It is blatantly obvious that continuing trickle-down policies are not working and the policies are not rational for Americans or anyone else in the world.

The economic cost to our society as gone up phenomenally with the Trump mess. The political cost could be the end of our democracy as we now know it. The more obvious to the common citizen that they are being ripped off the more visible the anger and resentment there is for the rich, the more the rich will rely on trickle-down policies to protect their wealth.

There is no societal fairness with continuing trickle-down policies. The polarization costs alone are insurmountable. Trade wars, death, and starvation are the early signs of a world economic meltdown.

Our only hope is to repeal and replace trickle-down economics with equilibrium economics.

PART THREE

SOLUTIONS (Rule #6)

Voters

If the goal in the twenty-first century is to have all or the majority of the voting population actually vote, then we should all have mail-in ballots provided for every election. No more waiting in lines at the polls and no Soviet hacking. Keep elections fair and keep elections simple without the Electoral College factors. The candidate that gets the most votes win.

Technology

Technology should always have the goal of making our collective lives better. Technology should be focused on making the lives of the middle class as easy as possible, as they carry the largest burden of our society. Not dumbing down our society. Out of control White boys like Mark Zuckerberg and his power to put millions of Americans in harm's way with Facebook is unthinkable and maybe treasonous. Taking Russian rubles during our election to run propaganda ads is a violation of trust and he should go to jail for his role.

Women

We need many more women to step up and take a leadership role. No other minority is in the position to challenge White males. No other group has benefited most from affirmative action policies. There are more women on corporate boards, in politics and starting small businesses, positioning themselves to take over. Women as leaders will be more compassionate problem-solvers and a lot more concerned about fairness and equal opportunities for all. We are seeing signs of women acknowledging this new leadership role with the "Me Too" and "Time's Up" movements. We need to see them work together and encourage them to step up and make a difference in American life.

Equilibrium Economic Planning

One solution is clearly equilibrium economic planning, seeking economic and employment equilibrium markets at every level of private, business, and government commerce. It doesn't take a rocket scientist, the pope, or President Obama to point out how critical equilibrium economic planning is to capitalist societies. It's the home of free markets, equal opportunity, and it's where fairness resides. You can find it yourself, in just about any economics book. Wealthy Americans and those who have made their wealth by using American labor are greedy and opposed to anything being equal because they would have to pay their fair share to protect all Americans. But instead, Trump uses lap dogs of the rich like Paul Ryan and spineless Mitch McConnell to protect their wealth by proposing trickle-down budgets that keep the wealthy from paying their fair share of taxes. The reality is that Americans could all live better lives if the wealthy in this country would pay their fair share of taxes.

Without a strong economic base, supported by having all tax paying citizens and corporations, the 2 percent will destroy our society to protect their own tax-free wealth. If the 2 percent continue to pay little or no taxes to support the "society of wealth creation," it will collapse under its own weight, greed, and ignorance. Societies and economic markets create wealth, not individuals alone, and maintaining a balance is universal and unconditional.

Americans need to impeach Donald Trump for obstruction of justice and colluding with the Soviets. If Trump stays as president, he will bankrupt this country much like his businesses, subcontractors, and other firms that dealt with him in the past. The problem is that White males and females were the ones who elected Donald Trump in the first place. Why? Because republicans are now using Trump like a puppet...just like Putin has done. And finally, Chief Justice Roberts needs to admit he is wrong in the Citizens United v. the FEC, because it allows guys like the Koch brothers and Putin to mislead Americans and buy votes during elections.

"Please, Chief Justice Roberts, admit you were wrong about Citizens United v FEC and bring back fairness, justice, and equality to American elections. It takes being about something more than your own personal pride as our democracy is at stake. Please stop letting your loyalties to the Republican Party take you away from our Constitution. Ask for congressional help in setting limits on campaign spending and fix or reinstate the Civil Rights Act of 1965, because it is clear there are few limitations for the rich and famous." (April 2, 2017, letter to Justice Roberts)

The Catholic Church

Pope Francis should implement a cleansing rebirth of the Catholic Church by expelling or excommunicating every cardinal, archbishop, bishop, priest, deacon, coworker, and helper that are by law viewed to be a sexual predator. Church officials need to work with local authorities to prosecute/purge offenders and protect the innocent. Have the offenders represent themselves in court and not be represented by the Catholic Church. The Church needs to be pruned back to allow for a new healthier growth in the future.

Priests should be allowed to marry so that they can make better decisions with God and with their spouses. After all Adam did have Eve and none of us will ever be perfect or without sin.

Globalization

The concepts of globalization are very dangerous and another extreme form of trickle-down economics. The idea of having one worldwide currency is wrong and would be unmanageable. Concepts like equilibrium markets and employment fairness would disappear. Just think about 1 or 2 percent of the world population being in control and managing everything. Given present behavior, supply-siders are mostly managing how not to pay taxes and creating personal wealth. For example, look at Greece: the Greek's were irresponsible with their own currency before the euro. Did you think they would be more or less responsible with the one-currency euro? Greece will let the other countries using the euro help them out, and are becoming free riders. It's disrespectful to independent nations and their citizens not to have the responsibilities associated with their own currencies. Most nations will be left with feelings of being out of control in their finances and with their borders during times of war. The reality is, trickle-down effects the poorest countries the most, where the divide between rich and poor can be easily seen. The US has been setting a terrible example for the rest of the world.

It makes it easier for our enemies to hurt us if we only depend on a few entrepreneurs to service the entire country. More competition in government and business is the only solution. When you have many providers servicing the nation, we are stronger against all enemies.

Student Violence/Schools

We cannot allow our students to come out of high school needing to "find themselves." Many of our Black and Brown students just find themselves in jail. As a society we need to provide a clear pathway to their future through apprenticeships.

Students facing gun violence is an American tragedy with no efforts being made to minimize the child carnage.

AR-15-style weapons should be banned in the United States and the US should implement a buy-back program to get them off the streets, with background checks for all gun purchases.

There should be no praise given to shooters for killing our innocent children and loved ones. Let's tell it like it is, these are cowards committing cowardly acts of domestic terrorism. As a society, let's forever refer to them as "domestic cowards."

If nothing else, we have to reduce and limit the loss of life.

Societal-Government-Funded Think Tanks

Like our economics, our think tanks have gone extreme and are misguided. Our think tanks are failing society in the interests of the wealthy. Because only the rich can afford think tanks. It appears their entire focus is on how to get more money using fewer people. How counterproductive is that when the world has reached populations never seen before? Where are the concepts of doing more with more, instead of doing more with less? We need to create labor-intensive jobs to hire large numbers of people, not intense labor automation for the rich. Much like our environment needs to stay green, our population needs to see green in the form of money and be paid for being productive members of society. When was the last time you heard an announcement from a think tank that made life easier for everybody in society, rich and poor? Our think tanks need to work for society and not just wealthy individuals.

Why is a fair distribution of wealth so scary? Apparently, either you are in tune to the concepts of fairness or you're not. Education is key and poses an unsolved dilemma. We have the educated rich and the uneducated rich. We also have the educated poor and the uneducated poor. It appears we have more in numbers that are uneducated and rich then are educated and rich. The same is true for the poor, with more uneducated poor than educated poor. How do we keep the uneducated population from getting elected and making foolish decisions for society when money decides elections? Think tanks need to work for and solve problems for our society.

Black Restitution

Black restitution is just an acknowledgment and appreciation of black inventions and contributions made during this American journey. Black Americans should be compensated for Black inventions like the cotton gin and others stolen by White capitalists. Some fractional amount of money should be paid to every Black American for items made of cotton. The world became a better place through the ingenuity of the human mind to solve problems using Black Americans. Let's get real, I would still take my forty acres and a John Deere tractor! I would take Black think tanks as fair compensation instead of affirmative action policies any day. We should educate our kids to the basic skills (reading, writing, math, and science) plus have our kids come out of high school with trade skills: carpenters, plumbers, mechanics, electricians, and jewelry making and the arts without threats, intimidation, or jail time. We like to solve problems.

Black American Think Tanks

Black Americans have to be more self-reliant. It's a shame that in the twenty-first century we have to be so focused on solving Black issues in the Black communities. Mothers and fathers in the Black community have faced racist policies, mass numbers of prison incarceration and, at the same time, being shot by police in the streets. Black Americans cannot wait for other Americans to help them. We have to turn to ourselves to solve our own problems and share our solutions with others. With God's help we can get this done.

Unite the Black thinkers of the world and let's get busy. The first step is having the belief that we can solve our problems. The second step is to come up with creative financing. To get enough money for a mission of this scope is going to take gathering support from countries and individuals with true wealth and an eye for a great investment.

Not many Black people have the privilege of meeting and communicating with those having true wealth, but President Obama and the First Lady Michelle have. I know I'm taking liberties to think that they would support and invest the time to lead the creation of this notion of black think tanks, but I just did and I hope they approve. I think American and foreign investors are needed. We need those that can see the benefits associated with these think tanks being successful and share our solutions with others. They will invest in black entrepreneurship. Black Americans will develop solutions in the United States and around the world for future generations as an example of fairness and equality. Our think tanks will have answers for humanity around the world. As Black people develop and plan their own American future and how they will be seen around the world, Black people will lay out a roadmap for success.

For far too long, Black Americans have looked to others Americans to solve the unique problems of the Black communities. It's time for Black Americans and their desire to solve their own unique problems, by prioritizing their problems and requiring their think tanks to come up with solutions.

I would like to establish three (3) think tanks, one in New York, one Denver, and one California to be named: The Michelle and Barack Obama; The Betty and Malcolm X; and The Coretta and Martin Luther King think tanks, representing the Black families that influenced me the most. I think we need a 1,000 people working to solve problems: two-thirds Black women and one-third Black men solving these problems as women are the superior species and should take the lead. Black women and men see and feel the urgency of our problems firsthand and with remarkable clarity. Black Americans are educated on feeling the pain of losing their kids and those they love to death, prisons, and drugs.

Using Black think tanks to resolve Black crime, health, education, and modern-day economics is vital. Black American thinkers are needed with the resources to solve the unique problems of the Black communities in the United States and the nagging world issues like the Israelis and Palestinians and North and South Korea would be the world's best investment.

We're living in a historic time and I have much hope for the future. I'm praying that I can interest President Obama and the First Lady in developing Black American think tanks. The goals: to amaze the world with our ability to solve problems and to achieve humane respect in the United States and around the world. We, as Black Americans, cannot keep doing the same things and expect a different result.

"Black Americans are some of the most resourceful, underutilized, untapped minds on the planet. We have been instrumental in shaping the successes that make and keep making America the envy of the world. Black American achievements have always been in between the lines of American history. We should speak of our own journeys, victories, and defeats and not allow others to exploit or to define who we are." (January 6, 2017, letter to President Obama)

As Black people, we have to stop doing the same things even though they have played a vital part of our history, (marching, protesting, not standing for the national anthem, and dying like martyrs) and expecting a different result for Black Americans. We have to do more, let's get real that is the classic definition of insanity. We have to think outside the box. We have to liberate ourselves to have the freedom we deserve.

We have to do this to make sure our society stays in tune with its own morality for fairness, equality, and shaping our humanity and creating a more perfect union.

DEFINITIONS

Antitrust:

A collection of federal and state laws that regulated the conduct and organization of business corporations, generally to promote fair competition for the benefit of consumers. Our focus has to be on fairness and competition.

Common Types of Polarization:

The action of polarizing or state of being or becoming polarized. To break up into opposing groups. Can't agree on a way forward. A lack of an ability to compromise. The view you support is the right view and you are unable or unwilling to hear opposing views even after presented with new facts. You're ignorant of known facts and don't care.

Some common types of polarization:

Religious	Political
Racial	Environmental
Income	Media
Economic	Class
Trickle-down	

Economics:

The social science that studies the production, distribution, and consumption of goods and services.

Exports:

Goods and services produced in the United States and sold to consumers in other countries.

Federal Debt:

The sum of the money borrowed to pay for this year's deficit and the deficits unpaid from past years.

Federal Deficit:

When the federal government spends more than it takes in, the difference is called the deficit.

Free Market:

A system in which the cost of goods and services are determined by the open market by consumers, free of government intervention or any other authority.

Free Trade:

A free trade policy that does not restrict imports or exports in international trade.

Globalist:

Those who believe in globalism and are interested in policies or systems favoring or promoting globalization.

Globalization:

The act of globalizing or a state of being globalized.

Growth:

One way to tell whether the US economy is growing is to look at its gross domestic product, or GDP, the market value of all goods and services produced in the United States.

Imports:

Goods and services produced in foreign countries that are purchases by individuals, firms, and government.

Inflation:

Inflation is a sustained increase in the price level of goods and services in an economy over time when the supply of money and credit expands faster than the gross domestic product (GDP).

Interest Rate:

The amount charged to borrow money. The difference between that rate and the inflation rate is called the "real" interest rate.

Monopoly:

A monopoly exists when a single firm is the sole producer of a product for which there are no close substitutes. There is an absence of competition that characterizes a monopoly.

Oligopoly:

Is a market form that is dominated by a small number of large sellers (oligopolies). The basic characteristic of oligopoly is "fewness." An oligopoly exists whenever a few firms dominate the market for a product. When we hear of the "Big Three," "Big Four," or "Big Six," we can be relatively certain that the industry is oligopolistic. The dominant few may control up to 70 or 80 percent of the market.

Production Possibilities:

All possible combinations of two different products that the society is capable of producing.

Production Discrimination:

The types of discrimination due to differences such as gender, age, sex, race, and/or disability in the workplace, resulting in these citizens not having equal access and opportunities to work.

Societal Fairness:

When the private sectors, public sectors, and the upper and middle class of a society hold up the living standards of the entire society and share equally the tax responsibilities/burden of caring for the children, the elderly, the poor, and the mentally ill. All must share the cost of our infrastructure, national defense, national debt, natural disasters, and war(s). Our entire society needs to be a part of something that is greater than ourselves.

Unemployment:

The Labor Department defines unemployment as being sixteen or older and not earning any pay or doing any work for self or others in the past week, as long as you tried to find a job within the last month.

REFERENCES

Introductory Economics, Third Edition
Arleen J. Hoag and John H. Hoag

Economics: Principles, Problems, & Policies
Campbell R. McConnell and Stanley L Brue, et al.

Macro-Economics, Principles, Problems, and Policies
Campbell R. McConnell and Stanley L Brue, et al.

Race and Economics
Thomas Sowell

ACKNOWLEDGMENTS

I started writing this book with the deepest respect and support for two men, President Barack Obama and Pope Francis. They took a stand against extreme capitalism and inspired me to do my small part by writing letters to those in power. Both President Obama and Pope Francis engaged in societal fairness while governing the masses, instead of their own self-interest. This is my effort to call out a rigged system and replace trickle-down (that allows cheating and lying) from being the law of the land. This is my quest to get the United States and the world off an economic trend that is unsustainable and replace it with equilibrium economics.

Our society needs to prioritize how and what to spend tax dollars on because we all know there is enough to pay for every citizen to have a good education, health care, energy, and a twenty-first century infrastructure with equilibrium initiatives. Most Americans are willing to pay more in taxes if they can get some assurances that all are taxed in equal amounts and abilities. Our tax dollars are being wasted on the wealthy and their selfish ideas of trickle-down capitalism and free trade.

CREDITS

To those who influenced me and encouraged me to write and finish this book:

To Mr. Joel Osteen: Thank you for your spiritual guidance. It has inspired me to write this book in an attempt to make a difference.

Ms. Sarah Wright: The first woman to establish a "Women's Ministry" at the VA hospital in Denver. She inquired about my relationship with God, for which I had none at the time. She talked to me a lot and gave me a *Good News Bible* and put me on my own quest to serve God. She is my most beautiful angel.

Mr. Kyle Knapp: Who would ask me almost every other week if I'd finished my book. He seems to like how I write and some of the subjects I will attempt to tackle. A top-notch veteran, I met at the VA Clinic in Golden, he still has shrapnel in his body. And to all the heroes that have served.

Mr. Kenneth Grimes: One of my best friends and a pure artistic talent. He writes, directs, acts, and keeps me very humble. Always willing to read my drafts and provide candid thoughtful responses.

Professor Call: My first economics professor at American River College in Sacramento. Professor Call gave me the confidence and foundation in economics that carried me in and out of the University of Washington.

Mr. Joseph Crawford: My grandfather, who set the economic examples for our family to follow, how to live, and what it would take to survive.

Mr. Walter Crawford: My uncle that taught me to keep bobbing and weaving and sticking and jabbing. To stay away from taking a direct hit. How to get, keep, take care of and protect your livelihood.

Mr. Robert Brown II: My son who will stretch my mind and my thinking to be inclusive. Bobby inspires me to make sure I'm giving something back and not just another taker. He has helped to make this book a true family accomplishment.

Mr. Adam Ramey: My nephew who is brilliant and understands the technology enough to help me finally put this book together. I cannot thank Adam enough.

Mr. David Hollis: One of my best friends, who did a great job of giving me great advice.

My wife Marion: The superior species in my family and love of my life.

My mom who worries too much about me and others.

ABOUT THE AUTHOR

Robert Brown a Black American economist is very blessed and was born in the wine country of northern California. He is an Air Force military brat that spent over three years in England and four years in Germany as a kid. Robert married his high school sweetheart Marion in 1974, and she is the love of his life. He developed an interest in economics while attending the American River College in Sacramento. Robert went on to the University of Washington where he received a BA degree in economics in 1978. Robert became a sub-contract cost analyst for the Boeing Company in Seattle and realized very quickly that he needed more education to get ahead. Robert went on to get an MBA from City University in 1980. Robert was instrumental in forming and managing the Boeing Company's only baseball league.

Robert went to work for Martin Marietta in 1984 as a program planner and retired as finance estimator, preparing cost proposals for the government. While at Martin/Lockheed, Robert was instrumental in forming the B.E.S.T. Organization, (Black Employee Support Team) for Black aerospace employees and families make successful transitions. It was the first of its kind. Robert went on to serve as the economic development committee chairman, treasurer, and vice president for the Colorado Black Roundtable. He developed the "In the Black" program in Denver to help get Black and Brown small businesses out of the red and into the black. Robert served on Governor

Romer's economic advisory council and was an adjunct professor of economics and business at the Community Colleges of Aurora and Denver. Robert loves God, family, friends, fishing, and playing over-age-sixty baseball.

ROBERT'S INFLUENCE LETTERS

Robert's Letters to Those in Power

These letters to those in power were written to US senators, House representatives, Supreme Court justices, an attorney General, religious leaders, and other prominent members of our society who I felt needed to hear some of my rules of economics.

January 22, 2014

Attorney General Eric Holder
950 Pennsylvania Avenue, NW
Washington, DC 20530-0001

Attorney General Eric Holder,

Thank you so much for your service to this great country and President Obama. Attorney General Holder, you have done an outstanding job of serving and protecting all Americans with our current laws in place. I'm hoping that you are still in a position to change the course of policing and the justice system in America to be more compassionate to all the citizens they have taken an oath to protect.

The incentives and rewards for police, attorneys, probation officers and judges to be right about everything they do has put together an organization of human leeches that sucks the blood and life out of any Black citizen that makes a mistake. We live in a world where police officers, living and working in our neighborhoods, can mistakenly kill Black individuals on camera and be free to go back to work in two or three weeks.

Where is the compassion for Black citizens in America? Are we only going to be equal when a few Black police officers on camera, choke to death a big White boy and are not charged? Will that make us equal? I think not.

It is my belief that the current police oath to serve and protect is ambiguous as it relates to public trust and accountability. The word "compassion" should be added somewhere in a new oath. Compassion, public trust and accountability for all citizens regardless of color or economic status should be our goal. We have to do more to alter today's outcomes and establish a new mindset for our police officers, our neighborhoods and our justice system nationwide.

Our world is different and plagued with some ugly new reasons for building strong relationships between the police and our communities. The mistakes of the Bush and Cheney administration in Iraq have created new types of terror groups around the world. Our collective security today depends in part on our communities working closely with the police to protect one another. Our communities and our police need one another more than any time in our history. Our police force appears to be a target of some of these new terror groups and lone individuals living in our communities.

Being non-compassionate while engaged in public trust activities is a deal-breaker for most public servants, but somehow the police officer has been given an exemption and it's wrong. Police officers and the justice system will have to make major corrections in the compassion expressed to our communities. I pray for your help to protect our communities by changing the course of policing in America to include compassion as a priority for every American community. Thank you so much for your service. And you are the Man!

Proud of You and Proud to Be an American Citizen,

Robert J. Brown Sr.

February 20, 2014

Pope Francis

Your Holiness,
Vatican City
Rome, Italy

I'm a Black economist, doing my part as a servant this year to speak out against inequality. I was influenced by my first economics instructor, Professor Call, who taught from a wheel chair with chalk on his lips and a passion for teaching. He challenged me to seek an understanding of the principles, policies and problems of capitalism. The shepherd's Psalm 23 best describes the love the Lord has for me. I'm feeling blessed and truly in God's favor to know that the two men I love, respect and admire most, the world's first Pope Francis and the first Black American president, will meet and unite against inequality. Your Holiness, the world needs you and your messages more than ever, and God does not give us more than we can handle. The world needs to be reminded that the first economists were theologians, and when Your Holiness speaks out against "unfettered capitalism," our world leaders should understand there is precedence for you doing so, on both biblical and secular terms.

Your Holiness, President Obama will arrive at the Vatican this year, creating what I believe are God-sent opportunities to alter the ideologies of former presidents like Ronald Reagan, that have escalated what you aptly called "unfettered capitalism." Supply-side economics is systematically creating inequalities in the United States and around the world. Something has to be done about the idolatry in America for Reaganomics and trickle-down money that only guarantees the funneling up of the majority profits worldwide to a few privileged investors. Your

Holiness, we need to encourage a global attack on the principles and policies of supply side economics by allowing laborers the ability to obtain the highest feasible and fair living wage from their employment.

Supply-side economists espouse free trading and lowering tax barriers that continue to eat away the middle class in the United States. The Reagan trickle-down policies of free trading have eliminated a consciousness for fair trading. To stop the growing inequalities in the US and around the world, fair trading principles and policies with the appropriate international tariffs are a must. Protecting all workers should be our focus instead of free trading, which only gives carte blanche to greed and abuse of our planet and God's people. Bluntly ignoring demand curves and only focusing on supply curves have over time rendered every worldly market activity completely out of equilibrium. Your Holiness, please encourage President Obama to do his very best to implement policies that increase government revenues to create jobs, increase marketplace competition and that fight for a "living wage" for all, especially the working poor.

Your Holiness' most obedient and humble servant,

Robert J. Brown Sr.
A Concerned Economist

July, 22, 2014

President Barack Obama
The White House
1600 Pennsylvania Avenue NW
Washington, DC 20500

Dear Mr. President,

My name is Robert Brown Sr. and I'm one of your biggest admirers for a lot of reasons but I think most for your courage and your ability to represent the best in what being a Black American is all about. I'm very proud of you, Mr. President, and I'm very proud to be a Black American. The world now has a better idea of what it might be like to be Black in America. Mr. President, *you are the man*, especially if Michelle thinks you are worth keeping (smile). Michelle was probably told by your family, like my wife, "You can't give him back."

The republicans have shown the world how to belittle and demean an American president and in the process have greatly belittled and demeaned themselves and all Americans. Mr. President, I'm writing you today because we also share similar concerns about the shrinking American middle class. I'm a trained economist from the University of Washington and became motivated and committed to reaching out to support those engaged in the struggle. Pope Francis was the first to speak out against what he described as "unfettered capitalism." So I wrote to Pope Francis first and prior to your visit to the Vatican in hopes of encouraging what I believe to be a God-sent opportunity to alter the trickle-down ideologies of former President Ronald Reagan, who knew nothing about economics but only how to deliver his "lines" just like in the movies. The republicans have been nasty in saying no to everything during your entire time in office, regardless of who got hurt in the process. Racism is being taught on the big stage now and their leaders are fighting to be heard. It is all ignorance; what else could it be?

I'll write a letter this year to a few of the most ignorant of your Republican colleagues like Supreme Court Justice Clarence Thomas, US Congressman Paul Ryan and House Speaker "Cry-baby" Boehner and just reassure them that historians are going to be just as belittling and demeaning regarding their ill-spirited leadership as they are currently being toward yours.

Keep up the good work, Mr. President. Keep fighting for justice, infrastructure, income equality, our troops and the United States of America.

Be proud and stay proud, Mr. President. God has blessed you and we should all be thankful. I will continue to pray for God's love and protection for you and your family.

One of Your Proudest Black American Citizens,

Robert J. Brown Sr.

P.S. For the record, Mr. President, it is my belief that if any US senators publicly profess that they "want our president to fail!" it is an act of treason. After all, we are at WAR, Mr. President.

September 15, 2014

US Congressman Paul Ryan
1233 Longworth HOB
Washington, DC 20515

It is my opinion, Congressman Ryan, that you are a lazy excuse for an American, even for a rich spoon-fed American. Your father raised you on Reaganomics and forgot to tell you that former President Ronald Reagan was an actor, delivering his lines. He didn't understand anything about macroeconomics and got it all wrong. In my opinion, former President Ronald Reagan did not hate the United States. He enjoyed being president and was good at saying what republicans Americans wanted to hear, but the policies are making American workers second-class citizens at best. American workers are the best in the world and many of the wealthiest Americans know that.

It is my opinion, Congressman Ryan, that we need both human and financial capital to make our economy work. Why do you continue cutting off growth in human capital? Your goal should be trying to get our economy as close to full employment and full production as possible. The failed trickle-down ideologies failed because it only addressed growth in financial capital markets—very old news. Whatever you do to one side of the equation, you must do to the other side in order to maintain market equilibrium. It's just a little macroeconomics and basic math, Congressman.

What a privilege you have to continue pushing the failed trickle-down ideologies of the former President Ronald Reagan down the troughs of Americans. And what a privilege it is for you, not to come up with an original idea of your own. Do you not understand macroeconomics either, Congressman? What a privilege to continue proposing budgets that you know hurt so many hardworking Americans and only benefit 2 or 3 percent of our wealthiest Americans. Be truly privileged, Congressman Ryan, and wake up in time to step up for the American people, rich and poor.

Congressman Ryan, your numbers game is misguided and ill-spirited. Even former President Ronald Reagan would tell you that. You know better but you're so privileged, that you'll hurt most Americans trying to hurt a president you have the privilege of hating. Hatred is driven from fear. You have an intense hostility and aversion to the president, I understand that, but as a US Congressman representing so many Americans, you can't control your politics any better than that?

What a privilege for you to think that you would make a good American president. Keep dreaming (LOL!).

One Very Proud Black American Citizen,

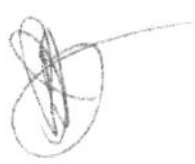

Robert J. Brown Sr.

October 2014

Justice Clarence Thomas
Supreme Court of the United States
One First Street N.E.
Washington, DC 20543

Supreme Court Justice Clarence Thomas, you are one very smart, tough cookie. You never lost composure when Ms. Anita Hill came forward with accusations that you had sexually harassed her. Your white mentors came to your rescue and you have been loyal to them ever since. I have always thought that eventually, Mr. Thomas was going to do things his own way—the right way—and shock the US Courts for all Americans. I thought this because you and your family share the seed of the Black American experience, including slavery. Being grateful to those that made a difference along the way is an honorable way to acknowledge and show thanks, but will the real seeds of Justice Thomas please stand up?! Hope and believe in something greater than yourself. Ask God to forgive us all for our sins—show unconditional love and be true to God.

I have watched how two of your mentors, George H. W. Bush and Ronald Reagan, used you from the very start of your career to do their dirty work of dumbing down Americans to sell their failed trickle-down ideologies as gospel. You became complicit in getting Americans on board to becoming a second class society and a debtor nation by sending American manufacturing jobs abroad—yep, the big Sell Out! You knew better, Justice Thomas. Was it all just for the positions and security and you just got caught up? If that was the case, you have no reason to be loyal to your mentors now. All you need to do now is be loyal to yourself, your grandfather you claim to be devoted to, and to the

American people, regardless of whether or not they are republican or democratic, which is the true role of our supreme court.

Telling White Republican Americans that Black Americans do not need any kind of help transitioning in American society is a lie. Get real, Justice Thomas: generations (300+ years) of legal discrimination in America, and in less than 40 years, discrimination no longer exist in America? Black Americans are now equal to White Americans in their abilities to educate and provide for their families? Wake up, Justice Thomas—no way is that true. Black Americans like me have been waiting for you to come out of your ill-willed, mentor-guided funk, and show the world what it is like to be a humane Black Supreme Court Justice. If you do that, we all will be able to say, "the waiting has been worth it!" Stop taking the textualist approach to upholding the United States Constitution and statutes and stop being political on the Supreme Court.

When the Constitution was written, this country would have looked at you, Associate Justice Marshall, and all other Blacks, as well as women and children, as the property of free white men. So please inform me, Justice Thomas, how can you take a textualist approach to upholding the United States Constitution and statutes? Seeking to uphold the original meaning of the Constitution is a cop-out, Justice Thomas, and your Constitutional approach to American concerns and issues have to be different! Show some unconditional love, Justice Thomas, in a way only you can or please just do us all a big favor and step down. If you can't be a part of the American solution, you are without a doubt a part of the American problem. Time and God will have the final say. I'll just continue to ask for miracles, and God's protection against my enemies.

One Very Proud American Citizen,

Robert J. Brown Sr.

October 31, 2014

Speaker John Boehner
H-232 The Capitol
Washington, DC 20515

Speaker Boehner, in my opinion, the American dream has been all about protecting and giving White males all the rights, including the ability to cry when any rights of any other American are achieved. White males fought for their rights against England and ever since have implemented legal discrimination in America just to protect your confiscated rights. Are White males so insecure they can't compete in fair an open completion? That is a big American problem, Speaker Boehner, that can only be solved by more education. More than three hundred years' worth of a head start and you cry when other Americans step up? Slavery guaranteed you and all of your thin-skinned White boys protection from any competition and allowed you to keep dreaming the American dream at the expense of others. How privileged is that, Speaker Boehner? You get to make all the rules and cry while you get to experience the American dream. How cowardly is that, Speaker Boehner? Do you love America, Speaker Boehner, and all Americans? Or is your love for this country only a function of protecting the wealth and privilege of your cronies? We all know that when the Constitution was written, this country saw all Blacks, women and children as property of and for free White Man. The love we Americans need most today has to be unconditional love, Speaker Boehner. Can you get your head around that?

It's my opinion that White boys don't chase dreams. They are the best in modern history at creating skewed democratic, capitalistic systems like slavery to protect their rights and dreams and will break down and cry if they have to share any of that American Dream. Americans' confidence in Congress has sunk to a new low of 7 percent for the first time since Gallup has been asking the question. Speaker Boehner, even I think you can do better but you're so privileged, you'll hurt most Americans while trying to hurt a president you have the privilege of hating. Hatred is driven from fear and you have an intense hostility and aversion to our president. Believe it or not, I understand how you feel, but as the House Speaker, representing so many Americans, you should be able to control your politics better than that.

Wake up, Speaker Boehner, and stop being mad at President Lincoln for freeing the Slaves. Thank God, President Lincoln and many other great Americans have been dreaming more inclusive dreams for America.

It is my opinion, Speaker Boehner, that we need both human and financial capital to make our economy work, so why is Congressman Ryan cutting off growth in human capital? Your goal, Speaker Boehner, should be trying to get our economy as close to full employment and full production as possible. That is not done by implementing the old trickle-down ideologies of former President Ronald Reagan. They failed because it only addressed growth in financial capital markets, and that is very old news with disastrous externalities for the American economy. Whatever Congressman Ryan does to one side of the equation, he must do to the other side in order to establish and maintain market equilibrium. It's just a little macroeconomics and basic math but full employment and full production requires market equilibrium.

Do your job, Speaker Boehner, in a way that all Americans can cry for joy!

One Very Proud Black American Citizen,

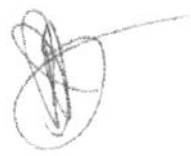

Robert J. Brown Sr.

January 26, 2015

President Barack Obama
The White House
1600 Pennsylvania Avenue NW
Washington, DC 20500

Dear Mr. President,

Thank you for taking the time to write me back, and I apologize for the cynicism you picked up in my July 22, 2014 letter. With so many cynical people these days, it's difficult for an economist like me not to feel the effects. I know you feel the cynicism too, but, Mr. President, you're doing the best job of not showing it, better than any other Black elected official in my lifetime. You and the First Lady are simply amazing. I do very much embrace hope and will continue to work toward brighter tomorrows.

I'm writing you today to say, Mr. President, your State of the union speech was one of the best ever! The new term "middle-class economics" will do more to make our tomorrows brighter than anything you have done to date. The shift from supply-side economics to middle-class economics was brilliant. The republicans are so lost that you have to be smiling from ear to ear. When middle-class economics gains traction, combined with your health care reform, our nation will be a better place for all Americans. Mr. President, thank you for your vision, foresight and leadership.

Every university here and around the world will focus on and define middle-class economics and move away from the trickle-down policies of supply-siders. Brilliant, Mr. President—I prayed you would have some more up your sleeves, and I would bet, if I were a betting man, that you will have more to come. Middle-class economics will be of great assistance in fighting for justice, income equality, infrastructure and our troops.

The State of the union has never been better, Mr. President. Your legacy will be hard to write—your impact on this nation and the world I believe will be unmatched for a long time to come. I'm so proud of you, Mr. President.

I will continue to pray for God's love and protection for you, your family and for this nation.

Sincerely,

Robert J. Brown Sr.

March 21, 2015

Senator John Sidney McCain
241 Russell Senate Office Building
Washington, DC 20510

Senator John Sidney McCain,

What an amazing journey and story you and your family have taken. The American people are proud of the stories written about how you served our military in the most honorable ways possible. It took a lot of pure courage to follow your father and grandfather into the navy. Although you did not come out as a four-star naval admiral, you have risen to become the Senior United States Senator from Arizona and your family must be very proud of your accomplishments. Please thank your sons and daughter for their service as well.

"What doesn't kill us will make us stronger." Your life experiences exemplify in real terms the spirit of what it means to be able to say that. After surviving the USS Forrestal fire and being shot down, injured, being a prisoner of war and tortured, you still have the desire to serve our great nation as a Republican US Senator. The majority of Americans like me have their reasons for admiring you and your service to this county but in my opinion, your desire to do anything and everything to become president changed you in ways that are very unpatriotic.

Winning at any price in politics can be a dangerous and expensive endeavor. You expect the American people to continue to forgive and forget the political blunders you are making as a so-called "Senior Senator." You call yourself a maverick by nominating former Governor Sarah Palin as your vice-presidential candidate, branding it as an act of being creative when you knew she didn't know her butt from a hole in the ground.

It is my opinion that your war against our president is offensive and disgraceful. You and forty-six other senators are waging a war against this president making you guilty of sabotage and treason. The United States is at war and in very sensitive negotiations with Iran and you and your Republican colleagues send a letter to sabotage the negotiations. You have proudly served our country in the military, Senator McCain, but as a Senior Senator from Arizona you have failed the citizens of Arizona and every other American citizen. Where is the spirit of helping our own soldiers, including our president? The best outcome for the American people, when you lead a group of traitors, is for you to resign. Step up, Senator McCain. Do the right thing and remove yourself from office. Your leadership is an embarrassment and you should never be allowed to represent another single American. It's an honor and a privilege to represent Americans, Senator McCain, but your political journey has been shameful.

One Very Disappointed American Citizen,

Robert J. Brown Sr.

April 17, 2015

Representative John Robert Lewis
343 Cannon House Office Building
Washington, DC 20515

I want to thank you for your courage, leadership and incredible service to our country—a country that has not always looked kindly upon you. Thank God for your wisdom and patience with a country that, at times, is unwilling to grow up. I admire your ability to maintain the philosophies of nonviolence, despite the types and levels of hatred that came your way. You have never let acts of violence keep you from your goals and your life story has an amazing way of depicting courage and a very strong belief in God.

Thank you for taking on the Black American struggle for equality and justice. Although it seems like we still have some ways to go, we are thankful Mr. John Robert Lewis made up his mind not to turn back and worked to shorten the journey for every American.

Thank you for fighting for our rights to vote. The civil rights movement was instrumental in liberating the hearts and minds of so many Americans. For republicans, protecting the rights of disenfranchised Americans has been like opening up Pandora's box. Disenfranchised Americans-black, brown, red, white, women, gays, lesbians and everything in between are now willing and able to fight like never before to protect themselves against republican attacks.

It is my opinion, the world is more divided than ever before and it will require the example of Americans to take the lead in putting their social and political differences behind them. The republicans are putting their own leadership into question when they seek to demean and belittle our president. Our president would be a lot more vulnerable if you were not there to watch his back. These Tea-Party republicans are bullying the rest of the Republican Party and putting the two-party system under a lot of stress. Help us all to mobilize against the Tea-Party elements of our society and any other group that seeks to limit the dreams of any American citizen. Help our president keep national health care and promote middle-class economics.

Your generation is proving hard to follow as we continue to fight for equality and justice for every American citizen. The civil rights movements inspired a generation of doers and thinkers world-wide, securing your place in history as an American hero. Thank you, Representative Lewis.

Sincerely,

Robert J. Brown Sr.

April 28, 2015

Edward Snowden
Federal Migration Service (FMS)
Russian Government
C/O Edward Snowden
Upper Radishchevskaya Street 4 D.str.1
Taganski District Moscow, Russia

What a mess you've gotten yourself into, Edward. I know you are praying a lot more now than you ever have before, asking for Buddha or God's protection and guidance. There is never a good time for a car accident, for a loved one to die, or for someone of privilege to become a traitor. I heard you were a pretty smart guy and you knew the Tea-Party republicans and racist Americans were not going to work with President Obama to repeal or change the USA Patriot Act, signed into law by mentally challenged President George W. Bush in 2001. Your so-called American loyalty and fears came to the surface in 2013 when you were able to talk a couple of media fools into publishing classified information you stole from the National Security Agency. How smart was that?

You know it takes both the president and Congress to change the USA Patriot Act; but you're smarter than the president and his staff as to when to bring matters to Congress. You worked for the CIA in Virginia in 2006 and were stationed with diplomatic cover to Geneva, Switzerland in March 2007. It is my opinion that you felt that you had to force our president's hand to address the USA Patriot Act in June 2013. You didn't even vote for President Obama, but you're so into yourself that you could be so disappointed in our president, enough to plan disclosures about our NSA surveillance programs? I think you could be a spy. You come from a family with a long history of being loyal to the United States and the protection of its secrets, so China and Russia more than likely targeted you. I'm thankful Switzerland is not granting you asylum, as you would prefer.

Ed, you're a smart guy. You think China and the Russians are getting some great propaganda and big smiles passing you around as the "great President Obama embarrassment?" Putin loves having an embarrassment like you living on Russian soil, but when his amusement with you is over, do you think you're going to continue to live the good life? You might just disappear.

I'm a Black professional who is very proud of what President Obama has been able to accomplish despite Republican opposition and traitors. Cowards like you need to come back to the United States, seek justice and take responsibility for your actions. Americans have a reputation of being some very forgiving people, regardless of your political or religious beliefs. You have a few here in the US that think you are a hero...but I will always consider you to be an embarrassing traitor.

Black and Proud to be American,

Robert Joseph Brown Sr.

May 21, 2015

President Barack Obama
The White House
1600 Pennsylvania Avenue NW
Washington, DC 20500

Dear Mr. President,

It is my opinion, Mr. President, you're on to something very powerful for everyday Americans with your healthcare policies and middle-class economics. The Trans-Pacific Partnership (TPP) is a distraction.

You're thinking and talking about capitalism in the US as if it were in a pure and perfect form. There's nothing pure or perfect about any "ism." If the US had a robust manufacturing environment and made huge investments in infrastructure and education, it would be better prepared for something like the TPP. As you know, Mr. President, that is not the case. You barely saved the automotive and banking industries. Your newfound Republican friends like Mitch McConnell would have sold American labor and manufacturing out to foreign countries. This TPP agreement will only allow republicans to accelerate the process of selling us all out when you're gone. I know you have no real reason to take a second opinion from me Mr. President, but have you asked Your Holiness or the First Lady what they think about the TPP? Does the TPP address the concerns of "unfettered capitalism" and give support to families? If one or both thinks this is not one of your best ideas, you should reconsider.

I pray that you stop your attacks on Senator Elizabeth Warren, because she's not incorrect about the negative externalities to the middle-class workers and manufacturing in America. The United States does not need more incentives to trade outside of the US The United States has historically been one of the largest trading nations in the world, before any incentives. That, in fact, was the lesson from NAFTA—greedy capitalists selling out American workers for personal gain. Mr. President, your focus should be on middle-class economics and national health care. Talk more about middle-class economics and the advantages it has to offer the middle class. Show more examples of how it is making a difference in the lives of everyday American families. Protect what you have worked so hard to achieve and take more executive actions when necessary.

Please stay focused, Mr. President. The TPP will just allow American capitalists to rapidly develop new American interests all over the world. Can anything rapidly done be well thought out? The TPP, like NAFTA, will be used in part to create economic wars not good for any nation, developed or undeveloped. Nation building comes from within, not from out-of-control interventions from other countries.

I respectfully disagree with you on your vision for American workers through the use of the Trans-Pacific Partnership. I pray you will have the courage to reconsider your presidential support for the TPP theories, that for now would only be harmful to the revitalization of American manufacturing and American middle-class workers.

Sincerely,

Robert J. Brown Sr.

November 17, 2016

President-elect Donald John Trump
The Trump Organization
725 5th Avenue
New York, NY 10022

Dear Mr. Trump

Congratulations!

Much like former President Ronald Reagan, you are successful in the use of the slogan "Making America Great Again" and like me, most Americans are praying for your success. With that said, I did not vote for you.

In the hearts and minds of many Americans is a love for Former President Ronald Reagan, because he made good on his promises to make America great. Every president since Reagan has continued to benefit by his supply-side, trickle-down economic theories until President Obama. Has everybody in America forgotten that former President Ronald Reagan was an actor and didn't understand anything about economics?

Unlike you, President-elect Trump. You understand economics and how difficult the art of the deal is going to be to restore economic fairness to middle-class American workers and workers around the world. You know American workers are the best in the world, especially when given a sense of economic fairness and the right incentives.

Long-term experimentation with trickle-down only worked for developing our financial capital markets and has done nothing, for years, to develop human capital markets. Both are required for our economy to reach full employment and full production. If President-elect Trump really wants to drain the swamp in Washington DC, get rid of House Speaker Paul

Ryan, because all he knows how to do is modify and disguise the trickle-down policies that maintain a rigged system against American middle-class workers. House Speaker Ryan is not your economics friend.

Equilibrium economics is the solution, President-elect Trump. Keep it simple: go with what you know and what you were taught at Wharton School of Economics. The equilibrium point considers both supply and demand curves and is the starting point for conducting analysis, making market changes and restoring economic fairness to American middle-class workers.

Good luck President-elect Trump, and God bless America!

A Black American Economist

Robert J. Brown Sr.

December 8, 2016

President-elect Donald J. Trump
The Trump Organization
725 5th Avenue
New York, NY 10022

Dear President-elect Donald Trump,

"Equilibrium Economic Theories . . . Making America Great Again"

Again, congratulations!

Restoring economic fairness to middle-class American workers is going to be easier than anyone thought. Taking this country and the world off of "voodoo economic theories" (supply-side and trickle-down economics) is going to be creatable and could be your cornerstone for making America great again.

The implementation of trickle-down put middle-class American workers in an unwinnable competition against producers and bankers. The actor, former President Ronald Reagan, was successful in "rigging the system." To make matters worse, former President Clinton took that nasty "voodoo economics" outside our borders with the implementation of NAFTA. "Really, Mr. Clinton, the Americans middle-class workers needed "Free Trade agreements?" NAFTA has no fairness in the deals at all for American or foreign workers. I have also respectfully disagreed with President Obama and his vision for the TPP. Both are harmful to the revitalization of American manufacturing and American middle-class workers.

The trickle-down and free-trade economic theories have done a great job of creating monopolies, oligopolies and mass collusion, leaving our economy lacking any fairness or true competition for American middle-class workers. American workers really relate to you, President-elect Trump, when you talk about draining the swamp in Washington DC, mainly because the best workers in the world are afraid and feeling unprotected in this rigged economy full of politicians that just don't get it. Equilibrium economics is the solution, President-elect Trump, it really is that simple. Bringing balance and sanity to our economic playing field, along with true competition, is all the American middle-class worker will ever need to keep making America great and singing your praise.

Good luck, President-elect Trump, God bless you and God bless America!

Your Friendly Black American Economist

Robert J. Brown Sr.

January 6, 2017

President Barack Obama
The White House
1600 Pennsylvania Avenue NW
Washington, DC 20500

Dear President Obama,

Thank you for your outstanding, historic leadership and service to this great nation and the world. Take pride in your many accomplishments and don't look back to second guess or think of any what ifs.

President Obama, your presidency is historic for many reasons but for the first time a Black American has touched and mingled with real world power. It's going to have a positive and profound rippling effect never seen or felt before in Black communities around the world. We have to harness that power, capitalize on it and use that power in a responsible and productive way for future generations.

In my opinion, as our commander-in-chief, you took a lot of friendly fire and some of your so-called colleagues are snipers and traitors that would have left our commander–in-chief, bloodied on the battlefield.

President Obama, thank you for your time in office, with the First Lady, her mom and the girls. What a beautiful family—we will all miss you. Your family will be in my prayers always.

We're living in historic time and I have much hope for the future. I'm praying that I can interest you and the First Lady Michelle to develop Black American think tanks. The goals: To amaze the world with our abilities to solve problems and to achieve humane respect in the United States and around world.

We, as Black Americans, cannot keep doing the same things and expect a different result.

Black Americans are some of the most resourceful, underutilized and untapped minds on the planet. We have been instrumental in shaping the successes that make and keep making America the envy of the world. Black American achievements have always been in between the lines of American history. We should speak of our own journeys, victories and defeats and not allow others to exploit or to define who we are.

Mr. John Glenn was a great American, no doubt, but I didn't want to wait until he died to hear how Black Americans were there every step of his journey. Black achievements and accomplishments are second fiddle, stolen and/or ignored. Some will to try to take credit for your accomplishments.

Thanks again. You're looking good with gray hair, Mr. President. I hope to hear from you and the First Lady soon.

Sincerely,

Robert Joseph Brown Sr.

January 6, 2017

Vice President Joe Biden
The White House
1600 Pennsylvania Avenue NW
Washington, DC 20500

Dear Vice President Joe Biden,

Thank you for your outstanding, historic leadership and service to this great nation and the world. Take pride in your many accomplishments and know that you are living a blessed life. The opportunity to serve at the highest levels of government during historic times, with the amazing President Obama, makes you one of the best Vice Presidents in American history. Not bad, Joe, for a boy from Scranton, Pennsylvania, or any other place in America.

You're not a Black American, but you now know how totally unprofessional and disrespectful your colleagues can be towards the highest office in the nation. You did a great job of not showing your frustrations. We all knew the strategy of obstruction, "no, no, and hell no," would never be a viable strategy to pursue as a domestic or foreign policy to benefit middle Americans. Ignorance and hatred still runs deep in America, and our most privileged Americans have gone extreme against the Office of the president, and indeed the president himself. Middle-class Americans are becoming the new American poor as trickle-down economics continues to create monopolies, oligopolies and free trading, all without tariffs or regulations. In my opinion, our commander-in-chief took a lot of friendly fire from some of your so-called colleagues, that are just snipers and traitors who would leave this commander-in-chief, bloodied on the battlefield.

I'll never be able to thank you enough for your service to this country and President Obama. I know, often you worked behind the public eye, and you were instrumental in getting things done.

Please also thank your wife Dr. Jill Biden for me, because when I heard how heartfelt and sincere she was, along with our First Lady Michelle, in supporting our troops, I became a volunteer. Now every week I get to hang out with some true American heroes. Thanks Joe, I'll keep you and those you love in my prayers always.

Sincerely,

Robert Joseph Brown Sr.

P.S. I think Dr. Jill Biden would make a great candidate for president in 2020.

January 12, 2017

President Barack Obama
The White House
1600 Pennsylvania Avenue NW
Washington, DC 20500

Dear President Obama,

You have a tough job, Mr. President, and our democracy has looked the same for a long time. Maybe it's time to take a slight detour for the good of the nation.

In my opinion, Edward Snowden did a lot of damage to US cyber security, first by providing information to the Chinese and currently helping the Russians to manipulate data and dissimulate it through Wikileaks. Russian President Putin started by attacking Hillary and already had compromising information on Donald Trump.

I can't believe what I'm asking you to do, but Mr. President, you cannot turn over the Office of the President to Donald Trump.

Please notify Congress of the War Powers Resolution because this is a National Emergency created by a Russian cyber-attack upon the United States.

President Putin will win this cyber war with the election of Donald Trump. The United States and the world will suffer unless you refuse this transition of power for now.

You are still the president and in this case you need to protect us from ourselves. Please do not leave us in a state of confusion.

Sincerely,

Robert J. Brown Sr.

April 2, 2017

Chief Justice John Roberts Jr.
Supreme Court of the United States
One First Street N.E.
Washington, DC 20543

Our country is in need of leadership and the Supreme Court of the United States sits on their butts and is allowing the dismantling of our Constitution while being loyal to Republican Party politics.

I think you got set-up with early buy-ins and you had no idea how much it could really cost.

Are you so sheltered from society, in your own little worlds, living the good life, with great health care, that you have lost your way to protect America?

Are you too privileged, like our president, to admit you were short sighted and made untimely deals when you gave the OK to Citizens United v FEC?

I pointed out to you, Chief Justice Roberts, the dangers in my previous letter dated September 5th 2015. Unlimited political bribery would lead to "those that have the money make the rules and win the elections." The problem now is the money is coming from the Russians. Is that OK or do you not care? Citizens United could care less about Russian interference, I guess, but I think you should care. This is not about just protecting your own white pride and privilege anymore, or is it? Do your job and protect the Constitution. Please stop being a Republican Party loyalist before money and power buy you and your friends on the Supreme Court.

Please, Chief Justice Roberts, admit you were wrong about Citizens United v. FEC and bring back fairness, justice and equality to American elections. It takes being about something more than your own personal pride as our democracy is at stake. Please stop letting your loyalties to the Republican Party take you away from our Constitution. Ask for congressional help in setting limits on campaign spending and fix or reinstate the Civil Rights Act of 1965, because it is clear there are few limitations for the rich and famous.

Sincerely,

Robert J. Brown Sr.

CC. Senator Michael Bennett

September 04, 2017

Senator Mitch McConnell
317 Russell Senate Office Building
Washington, DC 20510

Dear Senator McConnell

Senior United States Senator from Kentucky, member of the Republican Party, the Majority Leader, and the longest-serving US Senator in Kentucky history stayed in office too long and became an "American obstructionist liar" during the Obama Administration. You lied to your constituents in Kentucky in 2009 when you joined the Koch brothers and the Tea Party to oppose President Obama and make "him a one-term president." You hated President Obama so badly you wanted to launch another hate-driven American Revolution. Obstructionism is defined as the practice of deliberately delaying or preventing a process or change, especially in politics, and should include a close up picture of your face.

In the early years as a Kentucky politician, you were seen as "something of a centrist" according to *The New York Times*. Now you have moved sharply to the right, opposing collective-bargaining rights, minimum-wage increases and tax dollar spending that would actually make it easier for the everyday Americans. Your constituents in Kentucky need to kick you out of office. You are on the wrong side of everything Americans care about regardless of race including responsible gun legislation, campaign financing restrictions, and the Affordable Care Act. But instead, you look forward to holding Americans hostage to the lobbyist. Senior Senator McConnell, no solutions ever come out of your mouth, just trashing other ideas with no respect for the truth, fairness or rule of law. Where is the love for the citizens of Kentucky? Where is the love for your fellow United States citizens?

Your personal privilege to hate has made politics in Washington more divisive than ever. You are an arrogant, ignorant old man that has missed a unique opportunity to become an honored American Statesman but instead you, Paul Ryan and Donald Trump exploit minorities and women and pit the rich against the poor to start trade wars. For years you lied to Americans about repeal and replace Obamacare and you cannot come up with anything better as a replacement. Doing and saying hurtful things to people must give you an enormous sense of white privilege. You represent an America, that not many people are proud of.

In my opinion, large tax cuts for the top 2 percent will just go in the pockets of non-caring greedy capitalist Americans. These leeches in our society are very comfortable taking everything you give them to include the blood of hardworking Americans. Like you, they have no sense of political or economic fairness and are willing and able to change the rule of law and have no respect for the truth.

Your heart and mind must have been filled with hatred and resentment during the entire Obama Administration. I'm praying that you will find some peace... soon. I know God loves us all, even people like you, Senator.

One Very Disappointed American Citizen,

Robert J. Brown Sr.

September 29, 2017

Senator Bernard Sanders
332 Dirksen Office Building
Washington, DC 20510

Hello, Senator Sanders. Do you have any idea how much you have damaged the Democratic Party? You have single-handedly disrupted and made a mess of the Democratic Party, much like the Tea Party disrupting the Republican Party. If you were a true Democrat, you would have known how important the 2017 election was and you would have been a part of a one-two punch to knocking Donald Trump out. Instead you and most of your supporters became Independent Obstructionists. You are the longest serving Independent in US congressional history and you should have run your entire campaign as an Independent, because you are not a Democrat.

Senator, you were mean and disrespectful to Mrs. Hillary Clinton. Mrs. Clinton is one of the most qualified in American history to run for President, and this country would have benefited greatly with a nurturing woman at the helm.

But you thought you could win, and thought it was OK to get nasty with Hillary. You threw gas on the fire when it came to Hillary's e-mails. You wanted Wall Street transcripts of her speeches because you were jealous no one on Wall Street wanted to hear what you had to say. Wall Street knew you had no real ideas for making proactive or productive changes. Your only solution was to dismantle the banks with no real ideas given for how and why. You had delusions of grandeur, Senator Sanders, and you did not give your Democratic voters a way to reach out to Hillary.

Senator, you had a lot of first-time voters that got caught up in all of your delusions and they had no way of being successful. Like you, they became angry voters and wanted all Americans to "Feel the Burn" and as a result they voted for Trump or didn't vote at all. The Sanders and Trump campaigns were very similar in that they were both, full of mostly angry, uneducated, hateful voters. I'm 64 years young and have gone to a lot of democratic conventions and it was disgusting to be around Bernie Sanders supporters. The tone in your campaign was right there with Donald Trump, with all of your talk of a "Political Revolution." Whose base did that appeal to, Senator?

Your run for president became all about your own personal ego and not about what is best for our country. You lied about being a Democrat of any kind. Not even a Democratic Socialist would have conducted an election like you did, Senator. You walk around with that smirky smile on your face as if you are pleased that Hillary lost.

I think you are a phony and a fake and most definitely an Independent Obstructionist. You should have run for president as an Independent not a Democrat. You turned out to be just another old, angry, privileged, arrogant, White boy, doing a good job of slowing the American dream for the rest of us.

One Very Disappointed Democratic American Citizen,

Robert J. Brown Sr.

October 7, 2017

Senator John Sidney McCain III
241 Russell Senate Office Building
Washington, DC 20510

Good morning Senator McCain,

God put you on an amazing journey. I'm proud to say that I have been privileged to witness miracles at work through the Maverick, Senior United States Senator as you transformed to be quite the "Honored Statesman."

Your willingness to disagree with your party on issues related to party-line voting and a "return to regular order" is proof of your Statesman understanding of our Constitution. You are without a doubt a notable public figure with a long and respected career at the national and international levels. Congratulations!

In my letter to you in March 2015, I have to admit I was pretty upset with you and the 46 other senators for waging war against President Obama that I thought was sabotage and treason. But I felt compelled to write you again when you voted not to get rid of the American Health Care Act. Every American should have affordable health care.

Please call on Chief Justice Roberts to overturn Citizens United vs. FEC that allows those with money to make all the rules and win all the elections. After the last election the need for campaign finance reforms is imperative to defend and protect our Democracy. Who knows where Trump got his money, or how much to run his hateful campaign. Chief Justice Roberts is being too political and maybe too embarrassed to admit the Courts got it wrong. Finally, after the recent Las Vegas massacre, would you help propose some responsible gun legislation?

The everyday American citizen is being held hostage by monopolistic gun manufacturers and their lobbyist...Shameful!!!

Thank you, Senator McCain, for your life of service to all Americans. I will keep you and your family in my prayers. In my family you will always be known as an Honored American Statesman.

One Grateful Black American,

Robert J. Brown Sr.

Made in the USA
Monee, IL
14 November 2020

47605943R00066